MW00785816

Tom Eckersley

A Mid-century Modern Master

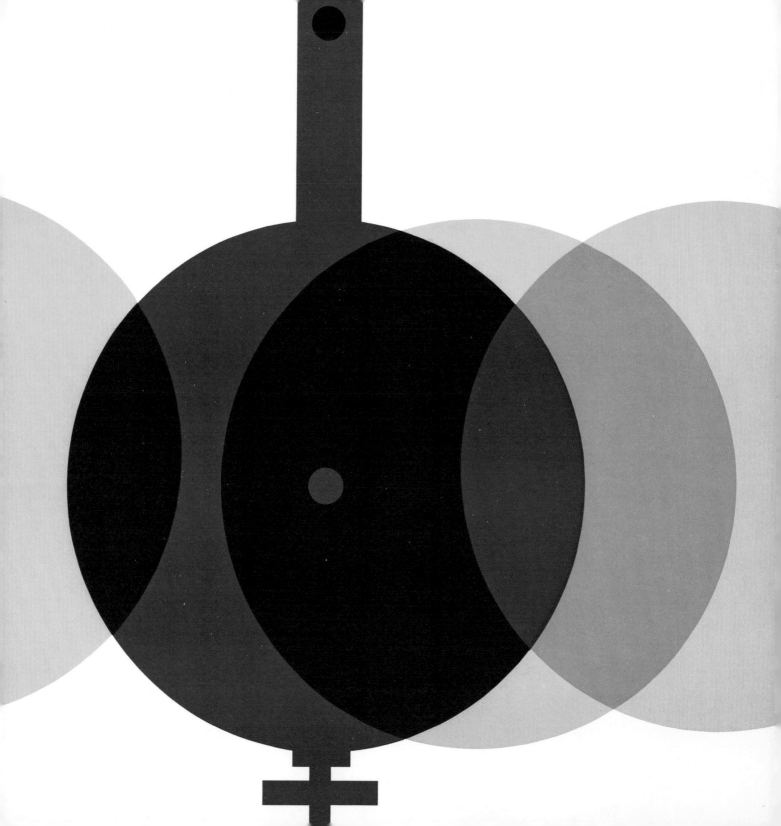

Tom Eckersley

A Mid-century Modern Master

BATSFORD

For Karen

First published in the United Kingdom in 2021 by
Batsford
43 Great Ormond Street
London
WC1N 3HZ

ISBN 978-1-84994-604-9

A CIP catalogue record for this book is available from the British Library.

10 9 8 7 6 5 4 3 2 1

Reproduction by Rival Colour Ltd, UK
Printed and bound by 1010 Printing International Ltd, China

Page 2 **National Business
Calendar Awards** (detail), 1983
Eckersley Archive, LCC

▶ **National Business Calendar
Awards** (detail), 1986
Eckersley Archive, LCC

Contents

Introduction

TOM ECKERSLEY was a distinguished member of an 'outsider' generation that transformed graphic design in Britain. As a graphic designer and poster artist, he also contributed personally to the explosion of visual print culture in Britain during the twentieth century. During the 1950s and 1960s Eckersley helped to transform design education in Britain. At precisely the time when the visual economy was growing, he was instrumental in providing a greatly expanded form of design formation, and to a great many more students. This produced a cascade effect that impacted directly on British people's lives, through the experience of new forms of communication and the elaboration of attractive new ideas and lifestyle choices, made visible.

The social changes of the late 1960s, combining counterculture and consumerism, were projected through the new print economy of colour-illustrated magazines, picture books and posters, and also, increasingly, through television. The image culture of the 1960s, presented in larger scale and in colour, helped forge a new optic for the late twentieth century. The new vision helped transform the perception of Britain in both local and international terms.

Today, we take the presence of intelligent communication design for granted. But it's worth remembering that it wasn't always like that. Tom Eckersley helped to establish the templates for intelligent and modern graphic design in Britain. One of the criticisms levelled at design, by the cultural commentator Peter York for example, is that *designland* has a tendency to speak to itself. Eckersley's work was always public-facing and was characterised by modernist economy (always conforming to the idea that less is more) leavened through the expression of a typically English sense of humour. The combination of a modernist sensibility with a light touch is well worth celebrating in itself.

The circumstances of twentieth-century economic transformation, political hiatus and conflict created a context in which the expanding print economy and the emerging practice of graphic design became increasingly appealing to creative sensibilities. Not surprisingly, the emergence of this new form of cultural production was attractive to outsiders who had previously felt excluded from the longer-established parts of the creative economy.

Nowadays, the émigré contribution to British design after the Second World War is acknowledged and well documented, and rightly so. Tom Eckersley was from another outsider group: northern, working class, and Chapel. Today, these traditions can seem historically remote, at least in contrast to the émigrés who arrived as modernists in the 1930s. The old-fashioned combination of a work ethic and the values exemplified by Eckersley's background played out through the specific development of design in Britain until the 1980s at least.

Tom Eckersley was from a north-western and Nonconformist background. This combination of geography and values provided a powerful motive for a form of design that derived from the blending of dissent and progress. Luckily for Eckersley, he found colleagues that shared this idealism.

Tom Eckersley sustained a career in graphic design for more than fifty years. His career began at a time when the term 'graphic design' was hardly used or recognised, and continued until the beginning of the digital era. Eckersley's success was testimony, against a backdrop of twentieth-century upheaval, to both his talent as a designer and to his personal resilience; and also to the qualities of his personality. The achievement of sustaining a career in a newly emerging part of the economy against a background of rapidly changing technological change should not be underestimated.

Along the way, Eckersley produced a body of work in posters and graphic design for different organisations that amounts to one of the most substantial and sustained achievements in the history of British graphic design. The first objective of this book is to share his work with a wider public.

Eckersley was a designer who was certainly recognised in his own lifetime. He received various awards and was elected to both international and domestic design associations. Eckersley posters appeared in the specialist design press from the late 1940s onwards and were featured in important exhibitions at home and abroad. This book acknowledges Eckersley's significance in the development of British graphic design and aims to account for the different strands of his work and to present it within the specific contexts that sustained it.

I was always aware of Tom Eckersley. As someone who was interested in the historical development of graphic design in Britain, I recognised his name as one that recurred, at intervals, from the 1930s through to the 1970s. Indeed, I was conscious of seeing Eckersley's work displayed on the platforms of London Underground in the 1970s and 1980s. When I began to take a more serious interest in graphic design and poster history, I was fortunate to meet him on a number of occasions, most notably when I interviewed Eckersley and his contemporary Abram Games for a Dutch poster magazine in the early 1990s.

Portraits of Tom Eckersley
Eckersley Archive, LCC

Later, I began a project that examined the industrial safety posters produced by the Royal Society for the Prevention of Accidents (RoSPA) during the Second World War. I started by looking at a number of posters designed by Tom Eckersley for this campaign and it turned out that he had been one of the principal personalities involved in guiding this venture. In 2016, the academic work that I had begun on safety posters was presented as part of RoSPA's centenary celebration. It's fair to say that, looking back over the last thirty-odd years, I seem to have always been writing about Tom Eckersley.

His personality was reserved but friendly. I remember that he seemed always to say few words and to choose them carefully. Quite often, he might remain completely silent. He had an independent cast of mind and had resolved, from the first, to work independently. This didn't mean that he worked in isolation. On the contrary, he combined independence of mind with a friendly and collegiate association with colleagues in Britain, Europe and from around the world. By virtue of his personality, approach and body of work, Eckersley's career provides a powerful example of how to combine life, work and design.

His reserved personality meant that he guarded his own privacy; the details of his private life are scant and he remains something of an enigma. There are few records beyond those of professional advancement. Nevertheless, the poster images survive. The broad outline of Eckersley's professional career was sketched out by George Him in 1980 in his introduction to an exhibition at Camden Arts Centre. Elsewhere, there is a partial transcript, compiled by Chris Mullen, of a talk given by Tom Eckersley at Norwich in the early 1980s.

Accordingly, this book is not a straightforward biography rooted in the personal detail of Eckersley's life; it is more a book that examines a life in design by reference to the changing shape of design in Britain, and by reference to the networks, contexts and communities that nurtured and supported him, and that sustained his practice as a designer. I've tried to zoom out and position Eckersley in as wide a context as possible.

The present interest in Eckersley derives from the stylishness of the images that he produced, and in his legacy of a substantial body of work. The poster images seem to have become more contemporary-looking with the passing of time. This suggests that Eckersley was forward-looking and, in design terms, ahead of his time. His work was always recognisable from its combination of a sharp clarity of line and boldness of colour, with a message lightened by humour, combining the better parts of continental modernism with a dash of British quirkiness.

Both Tom Eckersley and Abram Games remained enthusiastic and optimistic about the cultural importance of graphic design. They both retained their belief that design was an intrinsically progressive activity that aimed to make the world a better place, and that good ideas and technique could be combined with precision to communicate in an emotionally engaging way. Both were entirely sanguine about the advent of digital processes in design. Indeed, they believed in the primary significance of ideas and understood, even early on, that the digital would express itself as a continuous stream of poster-style pages, combining images and text.

Until recently the history of British graphic design had remained relatively obscure to anybody who existed outside the industry.

Nowadays, at the beginning of the twenty-first century, we can begin to see that the visual expression of the digital stream combines image, text, sound and movement, but that at its heart remains the powerful combination of efficacy and economy that derives from the poster pioneers of the late nineteenth and early twentieth centuries, and from the simple combinations of word and image.

Against this backdrop of digital expansion, the interest in vintage posters and graphic design history has never been greater. Indeed, this book is testimony to this present-day cultural phenomenon. Far from consigning the poster to history, the internet has consolidated the form as the source code and wellspring of modern communications. Again, this should make Tom Eckersley's career in poster design and education more relevant and interesting to those of us living and working within the expanded circumstances of communication design today.

Eckersley's contemporaries Abram Games, F.H.K. Henrion and Hans Schleger (Zéró) were from Jewish and émigré origins, while Eckersley himself was from a North Country Noncomformist background. This last strand of outsider contribution to design needs a little explanation, and the first part of this story describes the combination of values and enterprise that took the tolerant, outward-facing, liberal and enterprising identity of the north-west of England and applied it to the wider projection of British values.

In addition to presenting Eckersley's work over the years, the account of his life presented here frames his professional activities within a series of networks of people. The networks evolved and changed over time, the protagonists moved on; but Eckersley found, by virtue of his personality and professionalism, a role at the centre of this exciting story.

The outsider status of these early designers combined with the relatively small scale of the creative economy back then to provide for a specific community of design. It is to Tom Eckersley's great credit that he was able to move from one network to the next and sustain his career through a number of iterations of the British design industry. Part of this story is about the shift from the patronage of individual artists, associated with the 'pictures-for-business' model of commercial art, through to the more technocratic specification of design deriving from the necessities of the Second World War, and to the international and system-based design processes of the 1960s and beyond.

When I began writing about graphic design, I was especially interested in the perceived tension between continental modernism and twentieth-century British sensibilities. I was always surprised that it was possible for people to suggest that there had been, simultaneously, too much modernity in Britain or, at the same time, not enough!

It's been reassuring over more recent years to see how the specific and different contexts for design have allowed for a wider range of modernisms to flourish locally and to have been more clearly distinguished from each other. It's natural that, in the first stages of design history, individual personalities are identified as significant and that particular examples of work are signalled as iconic.

We now live in a society defined by a system of structures derived from the standards and consistency of property rights, legal precedent and logic. But we experience all this through feeling.

Design became a process that could provide an interface between this system of logic, in its material form, and our sense of the world through feeling.

It's a bit peculiar to be thinking, at the beginning of the twenty-first century, about problems that derive from an eighteenth-century systemic antagonism between logic and feeling. We just need to think of ourselves as parts of a long process. The huge development of technology has allowed for communication design to move beyond the confines of the print economy. We are entering a world where, thanks to the combination of technology and ideas, the activities of design combine to help us to begin constructing our own identities.

TOM ECKERSLEY
Exhibition of posters and other graphic work
October 22 to October 31 10am to 8pm
London College of Printing Elephant and Castle

DECADES 1935-75 **RETROSPECTIVE**

Five Decades exhibition poster
London College of Printing, 1975
Eckersley Archive, LCC

CHAPTER 1

North-westernism

The Modern Machine-ensemble and Manchester, the Great City of Progress

Dissent, Design and Progress

The development of the creative economy in Britain has advanced through the alignment of several distinct structures and systems of our society. In this chapter, I want to present a broad-brush account of the historical progress of this positive and constructive alignment. I believe that it accounts for Tom Eckersley's specific approach to design as humanistic, progressive and as an idealistic expression of human enterprise and effort.

This section proposes an alignment between the traditions of Nonconformism and political radicalism in the north-west of Britain in general and around Manchester in particular. In Manchester, the activities of manufacturing and trading laid the foundations of the modern liberal economy and also supported a form of radicalism that has, in the main, aligned itself with social progress.

The origins of graphic design are not to be found in the ancient languages that combine writing and picture-making. Rather, graphic design has emerged as the visual and technologically enabled expression of a specific set of cultural values that attach to a particular form of social organisation. These values are associated with both the organisation of industrial economy and with the machine-ensemble of modern urban life. The combination of system and progress derives from the emancipatory critique that powered the eighteenth-century philosophical Enlightenment.

The most significant concepts I want to introduce in relation to this developmental trajectory of design are those of the machine-ensemble and of dissent, especially that deriving from religious Nonconformism. The connection between dissent and design is more than one of historical coincidence. The dissenting tradition

Editorial illustration
News Chronicle, 1936 (with Eric Lombers)
Eckersley Archive, LCC

provided for a powerful critique of the existing institutions and organisations within society, and at the same time pointed towards something different and better.

The Modern Machine-ensemble

Joseph Whitworth, the great nineteenth-century engineer from Manchester, played a crucial role in the successful extension, through the integration of parts, of the Victorian machine age. In 1841 Whitworth proposed a general specification of screw-threads and fixings that became a national standard. Suddenly, the parts began to aggregate into something much bigger.

In the same way, Manchester's specific combination of liberal values and enterprise spread to a series of satellite towns across the whole of the north-west of England. The agglomeration of towns and cities became a visible manifestation of the nineteenth-century network of the machine-ensemble.

The term machine-ensemble was first coined by Wolfgang Schivelbusch in relation to the nineteenth-century railway system. The term acknowledges the scale, scope and speed of industrial machine integration so that the systemic and mechanical workings of the whole are given expression through this term.

As the term suggests, the machine-ensemble was formed as a group of connected machines of different sorts that each combined to form a network system. The network quickly became more than the sum of its parts and began to work as a meta-machine itself and form the basis for the emergence of a specific logic of machine philosophy.

The first glimpses of the machine-ensemble became evident within the Industrial Revolution of the eighteenth century. New inventions greatly increased production while at the same time reducing costs through much-improved labour efficiencies. The standard forms of machine-made parts further advanced these economies and efficiencies by allowing for an increasing interchangeability of elements.

The theatre of machines was quickly recognised as an exemplar of mechanical intelligence. Charles Babbage, the computer pioneer, understood that the physical arrangement of machines could provide for an automatic and logical sequence of productive events. Babbage describes this specific logic in his *On The Economy of Machinery and Manufactures* (1832). It took some time for the logical consequences of this organisation to become evident beyond the immediate circumstances of workshop and factory. The imposition of standard parts led to the standardisation of working practices and towards a more general co-ordination of elements across civic life.

The machine-ensemble became bigger through aggregation, but as it became bigger it also became faster. We can understand this through the evident acceleration of modern life as evidenced by the speed and stages of foot, horse, railway and internal combustion. Later, there would be jet-powered, solid-state and digital developments. Eventually, fibre optics would see things move at the speed of light.

Each of these technologies provided the basis for a step change, or quantum advance, in the speed and production of everything; including a specific image culture associated with the speed of the ensemble. The integration of elements and the automation of function that was implicit in the machine-ensemble changed the way that people saw and experienced the world. Society produced, at intervals, the new kinds of image culture required to represent the world as it was being experienced.

The modern poster, distinguished by colour, scale and the integration of word and image, provided for a form of communication that could be understood from a distance, at a glance, and while moving. But the speed of the machine-ensemble also changed painting, film, literature and music! In short, the machine-ensemble produced its own image culture to keep pace with the new technology.

It's worth noting, too, that the image speeds up in several ways: it speeds up as a convincing representation of the acceleration of modern life, and is also produced more quickly through improved technology.

Of course, Manchester wasn't the only place where these conditions pertained. But the scale and scope of Manchester's growth, and its long tradition of radicalism, helped to make this alignment more tangible.

The Making of Manchester (a grand city of progress)

Manchester developed in record time, and as a consequence of the accelerated industrialisation of the late eighteenth and early nineteenth centuries, officially obtaining city status in 1853. By the 1820s, it was established as a great centre of manufacturing and as the wellspring for a political ideology of liberalism and free trade.

For many observers, the development of modern Manchester was both exciting and appalling. The scale and energy of enterprise was exciting, while the living conditions of workers were frequently squalid. Friedrich Engels visited Manchester during the 1840s and described the living conditions of workers in his *The Condition of the Working Class in England* (1845).

Engels was guided through Manchester by Mary Burns and was able to observe the various horrors of child labour, the despoiled environment and the squalor of its overworked and impoverished workers. The brutality of the system he observed could be recognised in the many people broken as a consequence of unregulated working conditions and industrial accidents. For Engels, as for many others, Manchester seemed a portent of something both wonderful and terrible.

The historian Patrick Joyce has described the development of Manchester in terms of the normative structures, systems and civic organisation of political administration. This, he suggests, provided both the platform and bulwark to support the democratic extensions of the nineteenth-century reform movement. The great experiment combined, in the end, to promote a form of liberal governance and a connected form of specific social identity.

The historical development of Britain's great provincial cities has been well documented. Manchester, because of its size and success, and because of its association with both Nonconformist dissent and political radicalism, remains the most potent and significant exemplar of the Victorian industrial metropolis and of an expansive ideal of social progress. Asa Briggs and, more recently, Tristram Hunt have both written accounts of the spectacular expansion and growth of Manchester during the Victorian period in Britain.

Manchester grew rapidly from modest beginnings. In the course of the eighteenth century, the town's population grew several times over. The circumstances of Manchester's early growth placed it beyond the usual controls of democratic representation. By the beginning of the nineteenth century, its scale and prosperity had begun to demand a closer alignment between the material living conditions of the majority, and the regulatory framework within which they lived.

The emergence, from the beginning of the nineteenth century onwards, of new centres of population beyond the traditional boundaries of parliamentary representation required the reform of both democratic geography and of voting rights. The Great Reform Act of 1832 marked the first step towards redrawing electoral representation so as to take account of this. The Act also increased the number of people able to vote in elections.

The misalignment between the traditional spaces of power and their representation within the democratic process had been made especially evident by the imposition of Corn Law tariffs from 1815 onwards. These tariffs impacted disproportionately upon urban populations such as Manchester. The imposition of these unjustified tariffs on basic foodstuffs was quickly recognised as especially punitive to the energy and prosperity of Manchester. The imposition of tariffs was also understood, from the first, as being both unfair as a matter of principle, and as a flagrant attempt to shore up the prosperity and influence of landowners. Opposition to the Corn Laws was mobilised through the Anti-Corn Law League, established by Richard Cobden in 1839.

The opposition to the Corn Law tariffs soon became generalised beyond the original scope of the campaign to align both middle-class merchants and worker interests within its objectives. Manchester quickly became identified as the de facto centre of these new class interests. The violent suppression of the worker gathering at Peterloo in 1819 had provided an early and tragic testimony to the tensions arising from this emerging struggle for power.

In its early phase, the Industrial Revolution was slightly distant and separate from the London political elite. By the 1830s, the success of the industrialists, their wealth, power and influence, had made them significant for this elite. The northern industrial base was assimilated into the establishment, along with its values of self-help, free trade and co-operation, through the Great Reform Act.

In the end, the scale and dynamism of Manchester turned the city into a powerful symbol of both energy and progress. In political terms, the city became a physical and intellectual manifestation of a liberal, outward-facing and expansive engagement with the world.

Patrick Joyce describes the emergence of Manchester as a symbolic demonstration of a specific form of political economy. The broad streets, straight lines and improved visibility suggested a city where people and goods, and even ideas, could circulate freely and at the required speed demanded by the machine-ensemble. The city became cleaner and better-lit, the modern iteration of the 'shining city on a hill'.

From the 1840s onwards, the urgent assimilation of the northern cities provided the backdrop for a number of technical and moral standardisations. These were applied to the new social body, identified as representative of the industrial city and of its progressive agenda. These reforms took on a number of different forms and extended beyond Manchester. Among the most significant of these new systems and structures was the advent of a standard time deriving from the railway, and the elaboration of the Penny Post and its attendant developments in relation to street-naming and the concomitant identifying of individuals and addresses. Joyce also describes how the civic growth of Manchester combined elements of both expansion and control. The

MANCHESTER HEROES

main streets of Manchester became wider and straighter. It was within this context that the graphic expression of modern life began to be displayed and consumed.

The individual freedoms of modern democracy became exemplified by both the physical environment of the city, its panoptic and controlling organisation, and by the social body of its citizens. In short, Joyce suggests a relationship between people and things that is not simply one of practicality and efficiency, but

The events at Peterloo (1819), where troops charged a largely peaceful crowd, provide a foundation myth for democratic reform in Britain. The events of 1819 prepared the route towards the Great Reform Act of 1832, and helped to establish Manchester as a city of enterprise and social progress.

which constitutes the condition of progressive possibility and social potential identified as 'design'.

North-western Dissenting Radicalism

Looking back at the history of modern design in Britain, it is tempting to imagine that the emergence, during the late twentieth century, of a powerful creative economy has simply been a consequence of Britain's pioneering first-mover position in relation to industrial organisation. In fact, the origins of design pre-date the beginnings of the Industrial Revolution. The philosophical discussion associated with the English Reformation and its aftermath expressed itself freely through speech and through print culture, and the 1640s witnessed an explosion of short-form writing that could be printed economically through letterpress and widely distributed. From the first, the dissenters gave careful consideration to the visual appearance of their printed pamphlets and tracts.

Tristram Hunt records that, during the first thirty years of the nineteenth century, the Methodist congregation grew by over 200 per cent. By the mid-nineteenth century, 'dissenters' constituted substantial proportions of the total church populations of most large industrial cities, making up nearly 20 per cent in Liverpool, 30 per cent in Manchester, and nearly half in Bradford.

The radical potential evident in these proportions was discomfiting to the Anglican Church and to the civic authorities, who responded by endorsing a huge expansion in church-building and in Sunday-

(OLDHAM-STREET CHAPEL, MANCHESTER.)

The chapel architecture of Manchester provided visible evidence of the success of various Nonconformist communities gathered in the north-west. This nineteenth-century engraving shows the substantial central Methodist chapel.

school education for the working class. Nevertheless, the temper of the great industrial cities of the North remained more volatile than in the South. Christopher Hill, writing in the context of seventeenth-century English history, identified the north and west of England as a kind of badlands, whose history of warlordism had placed them beyond the control of the established church. Ironically, this relative distancing from control created the conditions in which both sectarian Nonconformism and enterprise could flourish.

The philosopher Herbert Read provided a twentieth-century articulation of these ideas through his many books espousing the moral virtue associated with art in education as a means and expression of progressive autonomy. His founding of the Institute of Contemporary Arts, in London, provided a platform for the discussion of these ideas. In turn, these inspired the designer Norman Potter to promote this form of modern British idealism explicitly across the art-school environment in Britain.

The specific combination of Nonconformist self-help and industrial enterprise combined, in the north-west of Britain especially, to configure an approach to design that was both practical and progressive. Furthermore, the tradition of religious dissent evident in the early Nonconformist sects was redirected towards social progress through the creation of a specific structure and sociology of liberal governability during the nineteenth century. By the beginning of the twentieth century, design, democracy and progress had combined to produce a positive energy for social change and material development.

A creative economy is not simply a development of a particular form of trading economy; it is that, plus an overlay of free-thinking that devolves from radical Nonconformism and religious tolerance; and from a form of dissent that is suggestive of positive improvement. These powerful traditions of thought and enterprise also provide a frame within which design is understood as intrinsically progressive.

Within the specific context of the industrialised north-west of Britain, the historic association between Nonconformist natural theology identified through both Christian perfection and free-trading, north-western liberalism, each aligned design as both an expression of profit, and of social progress.

The development of graphic design, facilitated through its associated technologies, has usually been described as entirely determined by the industrial organisation of society, and by the simple requirement to sell more stuff. We should not be surprised that organisation, technology and surplus combined, at the end of the nineteenth century, to shape a specific form of consumer economy.

Tom Eckersley had the great good fortune to be born into these traditions of north-western Nonconformism and radicalism that provided opportunities to channel his artistic talent into poster design. I believe that his choices about what work to do, and how, were shaped to some extent by his background. During the Second World War, and in the years after, Eckersley helped to shape a design practice that seamlessly combined process and progress. This informed his approach to design education at the London College of Printing, and helped form a generation – and tradition – of independent design in Britain.

CHAPTER 2

Early Years

Illness and Reading, and Drawing

TOM ECKERSLEY was born on 30 September 1914 in Lancashire. The details of his early life are incomplete. He was born in Lowton, near the small Lancashire town of Newton-le-Willows, on the outskirts of Manchester.

The Eckersley family were small-scale dairy farmers, at Laburnum Farm on the Newton Road at Lowton. Their dairy herd supplied milk to people in and around Manchester via the local co-operative society at Leigh.

Eckersley described his childhood as entirely rural. Lowton and Newton-le-Willows were just countryside back then, and beyond the outskirts of Manchester. In general, people walked everywhere. The local bus service only began in 1923, and the nearest tram service was accessible from the head of the road.

Stork illustration from *Animals on Parade*
The Conrad Press, 1947
Eckersley Archive, LCC

The nearest train was from Newton, to which you had to walk. There were very few cars.

Speaking in the 1970s, Eckersley recalled that his father, John, had been a great reader and knew every second-hand bookshop in Manchester. His father had been grammar school educated and had aspired to join the Methodist ministry, only to be turned down on medical grounds. This seems to have left him with a sense of disappointment and frustration that shaped his engagement with the farm.

We can only guess at the difficulties and uncertainties that attached to farming during this period. Eckersley remembered the farm as a slightly precarious activity and enterprise and decided early on that he harboured no ambitions in agriculture.

His father remained, as a matter of vocation, a Methodist lay preacher throughout his life and emphasised the importance of values associated with learning and tolerance.

Eckersley's mother, Eunice Hilton, was from a similarly independent-minded Methodist background. Her mother came from a good family that fell on hard times, and she took in weaving to make ends meet while Eunice worked as a girl in the mill at Leigh. Eunice came from a background that combined culture, music especially, with modest austerity. She was very sympathetic, and content with a life of home and children.

Tom Eckersley was the younger son, and their circumstances and temperaments combined to create a happy and self-contained family.

The family association with Methodism went back several generations. Eckersley's Great-Uncle John had been a minister in Ashby-de-la-Zouch, Leicestershire. His great-uncle was considered by the family as an eccentric and impressive figure with a taste for powerful words spoken with a booming voice. His great-grandfather had been a farmer and lay preacher, as had his grandfather. Eckersley recalled that his family were, through the study of scripture, used to reading aloud, and with good strong voices.

The house was full of books. These formed the basis for a practical, rather than philosophical, intelligence. Eckersley was not a strong child and spent quite a lot of time out of school, at home. The books came into their own as he spent time recuperating from various childhood illnesses. Like many children, he was encouraged to draw as a form of occupational therapy during his periods at home.

The historian Roy Porter has described the great transformation that occurred in reading cultures as part of the Enlightenment. Before about 1600, literacy was not widespread and most reading involved the precise interpretation of a few significant religious texts. Over the next two hundred years, literacy greatly expanded, as did the range of texts available.

In the days before the National Health Service and before powerful antibiotics, childhood illnesses could extend over a long period of time. Many days of school could be lost. However, if you were lucky enough to live in a home environment that encouraged learning, these periods at home could form the basis of an imaginative world that found visual expression, via books and reading, and through drawing. Technical proficiency in drawing was not usually encouraged or promoted in school at the beginning of the twentieth century so this proficiency, however it was acquired, was distinctive.

Tom Eckersley's background, with its combination of reading and illness, was revealed in the evident

The Salford School of Art was established to provide technical education for local industries. The substantial building was an important symbol of local and institutional enterprise.

pleasure that he took from the animal kingdom in all its shapes and sizes. From the beginning, his posters and illustrations made use of the familiar animals associated with his domestic life. Later in his career, his interests ranged more widely and a variety of more exotic species were featured in his work for the World Wildlife Fund during the 1970s and 1980s.

Eckersley's parents were conscious of the value of a good education. They wanted him to go to the grammar school at Leigh, or to Manchester Grammar School. His father even visited the principal at Manchester to request a place for his son and for a while he attended Lord's Commercial College in Bolton.

His parents were naturally concerned about his prospects. They recognised the difficulties of small-scale farming through their own experience. At the same time, they were unsure about the security of much modern employment. At first, they encouraged Eckersley towards commercial administration; then his mother saw something about art schools in the newspaper.

Salford School of Art

Eunice suggested that her son enrol at Salford School of Art and make a career from his drawing. He was successful in his application, and attended the school from the age of sixteen, from 1930 to 1934.

He was accepted into the art school without an interview, based solely on his parents' word and a portfolio of a few drawings. Looking back, Eckersley was a little dismissive of the application process. He certainly considered his scribblings to have been, at that stage, unworthy of encouragement. Nevertheless, he recognised his great good fortune in having been accepted to study at Salford.

The early twentieth-century art school was a product of the Victorian design reform movement and was conceptualised to provide a technical education based on the demands of the local economy. The local provision of this was therefore limited to areas with a demand for such skills. In Salford, the emphasis was on construction, chemistry, textiles and mechanical engineering. The activities of design and commercial art were, in this context, relatively small-scale; Eckersley was part of a group of about twenty or so students.

The Salford Royal Technical Institute had been formed in 1896 through the merger of the Pendleton Mechanics' Institute and the Salford Working Men's College, founded in 1856. The School of Art was one of its components, and the training in art and design was provided on the basis that most of the local students would find employment in the local textile industry.

The circumstances of the First World War and its aftermath had ramifications across the whole of society. Not least of these was that the great reduction in men, killed or injured during the war, impacted both on the economy and the social organisation of communities across Britain.

The patterns of British military recruitment had traditionally been based on local assembly. In the recruitment drive for the First World War, young men were encouraged to join up as members of local 'Pals battalions'. In the context of the machine war and tactics of 1914–18, a Pals battalion could be wiped out in a few minutes. Both on the ground and back home, the loss of an entire generation of young men from the same locale was a catastrophe.

The economic impact on a local community was obvious and required the replacement of the pool of male workers. Women workers had shown during the war that they were well able to fill this gap. Nevertheless, there remained important questions about the long-term structure of society, and the role of women. The loss of a generation of young men called into question the traditional life path for women, who had been encouraged and expected to find partners and raise families. Now, and in these changed circumstances, women needed to be provided with education and technical skills that were appropriate and would allow them to build different lives to those that they might have expected.

The emerging field of art and design was recognised as suitable for young women. Art schools across Britain began to address this issue and to promote careers in art and design as suitable for independent-minded young women. This strategy had the additional benefit of allowing returning male workers to re-enter their traditional occupations without the perceived threat from women workers taking their jobs.

All this meant there were lots of reasonably well-to-do and relatively sophisticated young women at Salford. Perhaps because of his sheltered upbringing, Eckersley was, at first, a little shy and diffident in the company of both women and older students.

The Salford school was forward-looking. The main corridor space had been converted into a gallery, painted white, which showed work from around Europe through various magazines: *Gebrauchsgraphik*, *Harper's Bazaar*, *Cahiers d'Art* and the like. These magazines introduced the French masters of modern poster design such as Cassandre and Paul Colin to students.

The focus on design reform and modernity was very unusual in Britain at this time, especially outside London. Looking back, Eckersley thought Salford better than Manchester.

At Salford, he became friends with a fellow student, Eric Lombers (1914–78). They started to work together on the same poster projects, pushing two tables together in a corner, working alone. Eric Lombers was from Manchester, and from a Unitarian background. He was very good at the technical side of design.

The principal of Salford wasn't a painter, but Harold Rhodes was interested in design and its possibilities. He was aware of individual designers in Britain, such as Frank Newbould, and of the famous names from abroad, and was an enthusiastic promoter of modern design as the style of the future. Rhodes had arrived at Salford from the Royal College of Art in London, where he had been among a group of artists and designers who were aware of efforts at design reform and the emergence of a modern style after the First World War.

Martin Tyas was Eckersley's main teacher at Salford and led the classes in graphic art. Tyas had the highest standards in his own work and demanded the same of his students. He'd give lectures sometimes and point out what was good in the world. One Christmas, Eckersley had been given a copy of the annual *Modern Publicity*, which was fascinating particularly because of its coverage of international posters.

An exhibition of posters from continental Europe held at the school had a great influence on Eckersley. Their visual impact was immediate and he resolved to become a poster designer. His application, discipline and skill grew and were recognised by the school, and he was awarded the Heywood Medal as the best student of 1934.

While at Salford, a number of key influences combined to shape Eckersley's approach to design, and to provide him with a practical example of how to succeed as an independent designer. Eckersley identified these influences as the artist and designer Paul Nash and the poster designers Edward McKnight Kauffer and Cassandre. Nash and Kauffer demonstrated that design integrity and success were not incompatible in 1930s Britain, while Cassandre seemed to attach to a form of design that was larger in scope and more dramatic perhaps, even more international and spectacular-looking. Together, these designers and their work began to point the way forward for Tom Eckersley and Eric Lombers.

Paul Nash (1889–1946)

The artist and educator Paul Nash had been appointed to the School of Design at the Royal College in London during 1924. Although the appointment was part-time and didn't last long, Nash had a profound influence on the group of students that he taught. He encouraged his students to work across a range of techniques so as to provide a balanced range of activities that would be mutually supportive. His students became poster designers, book illustrators and textile pattern designers, as well as continuing their work in fine art.

Edward McKnight Kauffer (1890–1954)

The American artist and poster designer Edward McKnight Kauffer made a crucial contribution to design in Britain during the period before the Second World War.

He was born into the relative isolation of the American Midwest. His precocious artistic talent flourished in his role within a group of travelling players, with responsibilities extending across scenery painting to sales and advertising and front of house.

Kauffer was persuaded in 1910 to travel westward to California. In San Francisco, he was introduced to the artistic circle of the art dealer Paul Elder. It was while working in Elder's gallery that Kauffer met Professor Joseph McKnight. McKnight quickly recognised Kauffer as a promising, but unformed, artistic talent and resolved to help, sponsoring Kauffer, in 1912, to study in Chicago and then to travel to Europe to advance his artistic development. The professor's generosity led Kauffer to adopt 'McKnight' as his middle name.

His itinerary took him to Venice, Munich and Paris. In the end, Kauffer's stay in Paris was curtailed by the beginning of the First World War. In 1914, he moved to London, expecting to travel on to America without delay. However, a combination of factors made Britain seem especially attractive to Kauffer. The general cultural atmosphere in London was more advanced and adventurous than in Chicago while, at the same time, appearing less obviously intimidating than that which he had encountered in Munich and Paris.

Kauffer resolved to commit himself to an artistic career in Britain and to stay, supported by his own efforts, for as long as possible. The response to his painting was not encouraging, so in an effort to support himself he began to search out poster commissions and other design work. A meeting with illustrator John Hassall, in 1915, provided him with an introduction to Frank Pick (1878–1941), who was then commercial manager at London Underground, and a man who would have a significant impact on Eckersley's early career.

The circuitous route by which Kauffer and Frank Pick came to meet is important because it describes the combination of influences that Kauffer brought to poster design after 1915. His beginnings as a theatrical scenery painter provided him with a clear sense of how scale, colour and simplification could be combined effectively.

Kauffer's instinctive disposition towards the scale and drama of the poster, along with his conceptual and artistic sophistication, was unusual in Britain. The combination was attractive to Pick who, as a founder member of the Design and Industries Association, was committed to improving general standards of design in Britain. Pick immediately began to commission poster designs from the young American.

Kauffer provided a visible connection between the hitherto separate worlds of fine art and poster design. The first artists to attempt poster design had, typically, simply produced paintings, or pictures, for use in advertising. Kauffer was able to develop a visual language that synthesised a number of different visual elements from modern painting into poster design. By producing, over time, a coherent visual language that combined colour, scale, abstraction, simplification and integration, he was able to advance the scope of poster communication beyond the prosaic demands of the advertising industry. Suddenly, posters appeared bigger and brighter and more audacious. No wonder they were impressive and appealing to young poster-design students such as Eckersley and Lombers.

In 1924 Kauffer wrote his *Art of the Poster*, which established the historical and aesthetic developments that defined the modern poster. This intelligent and rigorous engagement with the activities of poster design began to establish a new standard of professionalism and conceptual sophistication for the industry.

During the 1920s and 1930s Kauffer established himself as the most important poster and graphic designer in Britain. He continued to work for Frank Pick, by now at London Transport, and for many other clients, including Stephen Tallents at the General Post Office

(GPO). He forged an especially productive relationship with the artistically sophisticated Jack Beddington of Shell. A more or less continuous stream of Kauffer posters contributed to Shell campaigns from 1929 onwards.

In addition to the consistent patronage offered him by these figures, Kauffer was also helped by the support of Peter Gregory, a director of the printing firm Lund Humphries. Gregory was conscious of the relationship between modern technological development in the print industry and the opportunity for new forms of visual communication. Lund Humphries positioned themselves as pioneers of both technological development and innovation and also of design and visual invention. In practical terms, this meant attempting to understand how photographic elements could be integrated into the existing visual language of the print economy.

In order to drive this project forward, Gregory gave Kauffer a studio at the firm's London offices in Bedford Square. With the resources of the printing firm behind him, the Kauffer studio became a kind of visual laboratory. The studio was a bigger and more collective environment in which to work. The implicit direction, across every activity of the studio and its resources, was towards experimentation and problem-solving in creative design. The offices also included a gallery space where exhibitions of international and new work were presented to the public. These spaces became, by the end of the 1930s, the main entry point into London's creative economy.

Adolphe Mouron (Cassandre) (1901–68)

The great international influence upon both the young Tom Eckersley and Eric Lombers was the French poster designer Adolphe Mouron, known as 'Cassandre'. Eckersley became familiar with the visual power of

Cassandre's designs through the annual review *Modern Publicity*, and thanks to various design magazines that were displayed at Salford School of Art.

Cassandre was the pseudonym adopted by Adolphe Mouron in his career as a poster designer. The name is nowadays associated with a series of dramatic designs created in France during the 1920s and 1930s. He also designed typefaces for the Deberny & Peignot type foundry and was a theatrical stage designer of great originality.

Mouron was born in the Ukraine to French parents. His ambition was to be an artist and it was natural that he should move to Paris to advance his art education at l'École des Beaux Arts and then at L'Académie Julian.

His first efforts at poster art were greatly helped by his meeting with the Hachard family of lithographic printers, with whom he signed an exclusive contract. Cassandre's success immediately established him at the forefront of an artistic and intellectually sophisticated form of poster design. Working in France during the inter-war period also gave him a place in the most highly developed advertising market in the world. In 1930 he founded L'Alliance Graphique with Charles Loupot and Maurice Moyrand.

L'Alliance was a prototype artist's agency that pooled resources to maximise effectiveness in client relations and media sales. Cassandre's body of work places him as among the most significant figures in the history of modernist graphic design and visual communication.

His designs were immediately recognised as both commercially astute and intellectually satisfying. He was able to reconcile these often contradictory ambitions through the synthesis of image, text and art into a design that was a dramatic and exciting addition to the theatre of the street, described as *le spectacle dans la rue*.

The mixed-portfolio approach promoted by Nash, Kauffer and Cassandre aligned itself with the developing sense of modern artists as both restless personalities and creative practitioners whose technical skills could be directed at a variety of problems. It turned out too that, against the backdrop of economic uncertainty during the 1930s, this approach provided at least some chance of an income.

The creative agility required by this, along with the conceptual challenges of problem-solving across a wider scope of activities, were attractive to Tom Eckersley. He resolved to combine these various influences in a career as an independent poster designer.

When he left art school, he was ambitious and determined to be as good as Edward McKnight Kauffer, the major poster designer of the 1930s in Britain … and he wanted to see his work on the hoardings. At the same time, Eckersley was ambivalent about the prospect of having a formal job; indeed he was scathing about the traditional forms and structures of commercial art. The thought of rendering other peoples' ideas was anathema and he was determined to work independently.

At Salford, Eckersley and Lombers had begun to produce posters and to compete with the designs they saw on the hoardings. Their benchmarks were already beyond the confines of the school and they began to submit work to the advertising agencies in London, who usually replied with vague and non-committal praise. The two quickly resolved to move to London and to establish themselves as freelance poster designers.

CHAPTER 3

London and the 1930s
A Network of Patronage

THE 1930s have been recognised as the 'golden age' of poster design. This reputation is based, in part, on the acknowledged cultural significance of the poster during this time. Broadcast media remained in their infancy and the poster trumpeted its populist messages from the hoardings without significant competition. The other forms of commercial art – packaging, point of sale and print advertising (newspapers and magazines) – were, in contrast, of more local impact and of a small-scale format.

But this recognition was also based upon the evident quality of the design work of these inter-war posters. In general, the reform of poster art after the First World War reflected a more democratic and dynamic form of social organisation; the designs became simplified so as to keep pace with the accelerating rate of change of modern metropolitan life.

The best-known posters of the inter-war period were commissioned from the big regional railway groups, London Underground and London Transport, the Shell motor oil company and the General Post Office. All these organisations were closely associated with the accelerating pace of modern life.

Obviously, there were many other forms of poster produced for straightforward commercial products and services, but the great expansion in advertising was powered by the demands from these large organisations for images that spoke of both speed and glamour.

The poster was the first form of communication that combined colour and scale in order to be viewed dynamically, and from a distance. The poster pioneers of the late nineteenth century and very early twentieth century had understood that, for the poster to work on these terms, the various elements of the poster had to

Visit the Post Office Film Display
GPO, 1938 (with Eric Lombers)
Paul and Karen Rennie collection. Full poster on page 51.

be simplified and attention paid to how those elements related to each other.

During the 1930s the term 'graphic design' did not really exist. There were 'commercial artists' who did a variety of work in whatever style was required for advertising purposes. These jobbing artists were, whatever the technical merits of their work, looked down upon by the poster artists who considered themselves to be working at a more elevated level. At its most prosaic, the world of commercial art has been described as making 'pictures for business'.

Generally, the development of more advanced poster design during the 1930s was associated with improved processes of mechanical reproduction in its applications to the popular press and advertising. The increased use of photography, for example, with its implicit appeal to truth, was a powerful element in the developing rhetoric of the visual culture of this time.

In Britain, the political economy of poster production had developed very differently from elsewhere in Europe. From the very beginnings of poster production in the 1860s, the British cultural establishment took an ambivalent, if not hostile, view of this metropolitan manifestation of industrial capitalism and materialist consumption, and the display of advertising material was strictly controlled from the start. The principal instruments of this control were by-laws that controlled the display of advertising material and that, simultaneously, promoted the development of an economy of poster display structured by the relative scarcity of authorised poster sites. The usual laws of supply and demand were soon in operation, so that poster advertising quickly became priced beyond the scope of any but the largest concerns.

The poster was the undisputed summit of advertising in the period before the Second World War. The large scale of the work was, along with its public display, a sign of its significance. Furthermore, the combination of craft skills and fine art aesthetics within the design characterised the tasteful poster of the 1930s and allowed poster artists to claim some link to the high culture of gallery painting.

It was evident to both Eckersley and Lombers that, in order to make a go of poster-designing, they would have to be in London where they could meet the new patrons of advertising and develop their contacts. Sensibly, they had made two special fact-finding visits to London while still students at Salford. Based on the favourable reception they received, they resolved to move to the capital upon leaving Salford School of Art. It was therefore into this competitive environment that Eckersley and Lombers plunged during 1934.

The pair immediately began to submit designs to prospective clients. Eckersley's family were broadly supportive, on the condition that if the outlook after six months was not promising, the two designers would return to Manchester. The family advice was to be cautious and to eschew the complications of freelance work and accept positions with a commercial studio. But both men had set their minds on working independently. However, there followed a hard period of seven weeks without receiving a commission.

During the 1930s, the most successful poster designers worked for their own account and from their own studios. The concept of the multi-disciplinary creative studio had not yet been completely developed. It would emerge out of the scaling up of enterprise and provision that were a consequence of the war economy during the 1940s. The design economy would also be further boosted by the massive expansion in the scale and scope of government activities as part of post-war rebuilding.

Eckersley and Lombers rented two rooms in a house run by a French landlady on Ebury Street, close to the Victoria railway terminus. Despite its relatively grand location on the fringes of Belgravia, the street offered inexpensive lodgings in a convenient location. The studio was conveniently placed for visits to the London Transport headquarters in Westminster and to the office of Frank Pick, and for the Westminster School of Art where the pair taught the poster class through the 1930s. They used one of their rooms as a studio and the other to sleep in, and remained there throughout the 1930s and right up to the start of the war, when the Eckersley-Lombers professional partnership was dissolved.

In the beginning, and as at Salford, Eckersley and Lombers were working out the process of design for each project as they went along. There didn't seem to be a single way of doing things, and the process by which designs were thought up and elaborated upon depended on both personality and preference, but it was important to have someone to bounce ideas off. In the end, it seemed to come down to whatever worked and the say-so of a handful of patrons. Other designers who worked together, Lewitt-Him (Jan Le Witt and George Him) for example, also worked in a similar way, by dividing up the work. From the middle of the 1930s, being independent didn't mean being isolated. The model for the creative studio was beginning to develop as a space in which several people could collaborate in both the execution of the work and its conceptual elaboration.

Eckersley, who would often work late, would start the day by casting a fresh eye over his work and correcting anything that wasn't quite right.

We don't have a precise idea of how the two men divided their work, but Eckersley recalled that Lombers was very good at lettering. Nowadays, we are familiar with an extraordinary variety of letterforms, on both a small and large scale. In the 1930s, however, and especially in relation to poster-scale work, the letters were generally drawn out and positioned in relation to each other as part of the design.

The modern development of typography, like the poster itself, was closely linked to the acceleration of modern life. The elaboration of large poster-scale lettering was, during the early history of poster design, a variation and combination of geometry and drawing; unsurprisingly, the results were often of mixed quality. Slabs, strokes and weight combined, for example in art-deco styling, to create a rather architectural and overbearing geometry within the letters of many posters. As a response to this, at London Transport and the London and North Eastern Railway specific forms of sans serif were elaborated, by Edward Johnston (London Underground's Johnston font) and Eric Gill (Gill Sans) respectively, to express a coherent and consistent message across the entire range of these networked systems.

Patrons of the Poster

Technological development and social change, deriving from a combination of reform and recession, had produced an environment during the 1930s when design reform was entering a second phase, and embracing the machine-ensemble to expand and accelerate its activities of production and communication.

The design reform movement, founded by nineteenth-century radicals, had espoused the moral improvement of society through an association with the hand-made and the authentic. By the early twentieth century it had become clear that the moral benefits deriving from exquisite objects could not realise the mass-market potential for change unless they were mass-produced. The idealism of the first reformers was replaced by a pragmatic embrace of the benefits of mechanical production and of the machine process. Furthermore, the second wave of design reformers were very much more scientific in their approach, embracing the collection of quantifiable evidence, of sales for example, to support their activities.

The period after the First World War also witnessed the emergence of a number of very much larger organisations whose command-and-control structures were derived from the military organisation of the First World War.

In these circumstances, young designers were confronted with a design economy in which a few significant players were connected, by virtue of their activities and organisations, into a small network of personal patronage.

London Transport

The early association between Eckersley-Lombers and London Transport (and also the GPO) brought the young designers into contact with some of the most important and influential personalities in the British design establishment.

London Transport had a reputation as the most important organisation of patronage in poster design. Harold Rhodes, Eckersley's principal at Salford, had provided the pair with an introduction to Frank Pick,

who agreed to look at their portfolio. The young designers were then summoned, upon their arrival in London, to see Christian Barman at the Westminster offices of the organisation.

They were already familiar with London Transport posters via the magazine Art and Industry. The clarity and simplicity of the posters was interesting and contrasted with the relative complexity and confusion of much commercial art. The London Transport material seemed different from all the other posters on the hoardings. Eckersley and Lombers were also impressed by their being more like the continental posters that they admired.

London Transport posters were shown in sets both outside stations and inside on the platforms and corridors. Frank Pick had organised the displays so that they were tidy and coherent, like a gallery. The posters were all over London so it was also good publicity for Eckersley and Lombers.

From the first meeting onwards Eckersley and Lombers would usually deal, in the first instance, with Christian Barman, who had been appointed publicity manager at London Transport in 1935. He had been editor of The Architectural Review and Frank Pick had recruited him. In practice this meant that he worked side by side with Frank Pick. Barman's office would call the studio and request a visit from the designers. Barman would describe the brief over tea and the designers would return to their studio to begin work. A second meeting was called to view the resulting design. Barman would always consult with Pick, who insisted on seeing all the designs for himself.

Eckersley-Lombers always supplied full-sized artwork with hand-drawn lettering for their poster design submissions. Barman treated the artists and designers exceptionally well. There wasn't much contact, but it was very rare to have something rejected outright. Subsequent commissions came from people seeing work at London Transport stations and within the buses, trains and trams of the network.

Barman conceptualised a smaller-format poster, called a panel poster, which could be displayed within the interior of an underground carriage, bus or tram. These posters were generally linked to a specific event within the London calendar: exhibitions at Earl's Court or Olympia, sporting events and suchlike. The interior display of these posters provided a different context for these designs. The smaller format of the posters was both economic to produce and ubiquitous in its display. The number of interior sites required print runs of thousands for these panel posters, compared with the few hundred printed of the larger posters for display on platform sites.

The panel posters were a convenient and beneficial format for both publisher and designer. The designer received a maximum of exposure due to the very much larger print run, while the publisher reduced the financial risks associated with short-run and large-scale poster printing. Furthermore, the designers also gained from the explicit association, evident in the panel posters, with the cultural life and pageantry of London.

During the 1930s, the London Transport panel poster also provided a space in which designers could experiment with the integration of photographic elements into the established visual language of poster design. The records show that during the 1930s panel poster commissions from London Transport provided a consistent and substantial flow of work for Tom Eckersley and Eric Lombers.

The successful association with London Transport immediately established the duo among the top echelon of poster designers in Britain during the 1930s. This position was further enhanced by the appearance, at regular intervals during the decade, of poster designs by Eckersley-Lombers among the selections made by design publications *Art and Industry*, *Commercial Art* and *Modern Publicity*.

Frank Pick was one of the most important personalities in the history of design in Britain, and a few words need to be said about him. He was not a designer but an administrator of genius who conceived the idea of an integrated transport system comprising buses, trams and underground railways serving the whole metropolitan area of London.

Frank Pick was the most important and significant figure among the new patrons of poster art. He was born in Spalding, Lincolnshire, and raised in York where he attended school and chapel. The Nonconformist background of the Salem chapel formed Pick's fastidious sense of moral conscience and social duty.

In 1903, Pick took a job with the North Eastern Railway, whose headquarters were in York, in their newly established traffic statistics office. The NER was not the largest of railway companies, but it had a reputation for efficiency and progressive management. Pick was later appointed assistant to the general manager, George Gibb, and when Gibb was headhunted in 1905 to take charge of the Underground Electric Railways of London (UERL), Pick was invited to join him in London. The underground railways were in a difficult position: modernisation and new building had greatly indebted the firm. Gibb's task was to stabilise the financial situation and to increase traffic on the new lines.

Gibb also appointed Albert Stanley to the company. Stanley, later Lord Ashfield, was an American transport manager with an astute appreciation of the value of marketing and public relations. Pick realised, from the very first, that the financial situation and marketing were connected. The poor levels of trade were, in some sense, an indictment of the company's publicity. Pick was invited to improve upon this situation and in 1908 Stanley gave him complete responsibility for all the UERL's publicity.

Pick's background and influences combined to give him a meticulous approach to business analysis and, at the same time, allowed him to see the broader, more expansive picture. This meant he was able to align and integrate the various activities of the business as it expanded. He began to conceptualise the advertising of the expanded group so as to integrate and co-ordinate the different services. This integration was expressed through a more consistent graphic style in its communication with the public.

The first building block of this process was to find a typeface that could be used, across all the buildings of the system, for each of the wide variety of communications required by the organisation. Pick commissioned Edward Johnston to create a clear and easy-to-read typeface for the UERL in 1913. Pick's brief was a letterform suitable for signage. Within the specific context of the underground and its environments it was especially important that the resulting signage should be clearly legible. Obviously, it was equally important that the signage should contribute to the smooth flows of large numbers of people.

There was a further expansion of the UERL throughout the 1920s and 1930s as the Northern, Central and Piccadilly lines were each extended. The suburban expansion of the system allowed, from the start, for a combination of architecture, lettering and signage that was consistent and progressive.

In 1928 Pick was made managing director of the company and in 1933, the UERL became subsumed into a single, unified, public authority named the London Passenger Transport Board. The LPTB was later renamed London Transport.

Speaking to the Royal Society of Arts, in 1935, Pick described his activities:

> … beneath all the commercial activities of the Board, underneath all its engineering and operation, there is the revelation and realisation of something which is in the nature of a work of art … it is, in fact, a conception of the metropolis as a centre of life, of civilisation; more intense, more eager, more vitalising, than has ever so far obtained.

The association between design, progress and improvement described by Pick was characteristic of the design reform movement of the 1920s and 1930s. The lessons of Arts and Crafts design reform were that, without economy and convenience, the provision of goods and services could only be assured to a small and wealthy elite.

Pick understood that the accelerating expansion of the metropolis, facilitated by his own organisation, created a palpable anxiety among some of its citizens. The flux and speed of modernity was as destabilising as it was exciting. Nowhere was this more evident than in the constricted environments of the underground stations. In such locations, the posters were there primarily to provide information and direction. A good poster distinguished itself, believed Pick, by being useful.

The poster environment conceptualised by Pick became the expression of something practical, safe and harmonious. The poster helped normalise the unusual behaviour of going deep beneath the surface of the streets. It was even possible to imagine that the pictorial alignment of images, along the platforms of underground stations, became for many passengers a vista, more dynamic or poetic depending on the direction of travel, between the comforts of rest or the excitements of metropolitan pleasure.

It was entirely natural that Frank Pick should have been a founder member of the Design and Industries Association in 1915. His achievements at the UERL by then were already substantial and Pick was immediately recognised as a senior figure within the DIA. The esteem and respect in which he was held were reflected in his appointment as President of the DIA in 1928 and as Chairman of the Council for Industrial Design in 1934. Pick rejected the public honours that were offered to him.

In 1940, Pick left London Transport. His wartime appointment as director general of the Ministry of Information was short-lived. He retired, in ill health, and died at his home in 1941. In 1942, and as part of an appreciation published in *The Architectural Review*, Nikolaus Pevsner, the émigré architectural historian, described him as 'a modern Medici'.

The records at London Transport show that Eckersley-Lombers enjoyed the consistent patronage of Frank Pick. By the end of the decade they had contributed some 36 posters to the London Transport campaign on a wide variety of themes.

Stephen Tallents (1884–1958) and John Grierson (1898–1972)

In 1926, Frank Pick had been invited to chair the Publicity Committee of the newly formed Empire Marketing Board (EMB). The board, under the stewardship of Sir Stephen Tallents, had been an attempt to manage, in terms of public relations, the issue of trade and commerce across the British Empire. The EMB was established to promote trading relations, at consumer and wholesale levels, between Britain and the Empire.

The task was familiar to Pick. The economic benefits and practical convenience of imperial trading relations had to be made evident to many people for whom, and for whatever reason, the origins of products remained mysterious. It is not surprising that, having understood the task as one of informing and educating, Tallents and Pick should conceptualise a series of educational posters and prints.

In addition to the poster images, Tallents was quick to recognise the potential of cinema for public relations. He established the Empire Film Unit, under the technical guidance of John Grierson, and began to make documentary films about the peoples and communities of Empire.

Grierson had gone to North America in 1924 to study the pioneering work of Walter Lippmann and Edward Bernays in public relations. Lippmann was famously sceptical about the possibilities of the ordinary person being able, within the workings of mass democracy, to make an informed judgement about the complex and varied problems of policy.

The entrenched cynicism implicit in Lippmann's view provoked Grierson to address the problem of public relations through information and education. Following a suggestion from Lippman, Grierson began to investigate film and cinema as a way of addressing the problems of mass communications. Grierson immersed himself in the film and cinema industry at a time of rapid and ceaseless experimentation. He became aware of the documentary experiments of Robert Flaherty through his film *Nanook of the North* (1922) and also of the Soviet experiments of Sergei Eisenstein, and Dziga Vertov's *Man with a Movie Camera* (1929).

When Grierson returned to the UK in 1927, he approached the EMB with a view to developing his ideas about mass communication. Tallents had already begun to use films to promote the EMB's ideas to young children. He recognised, however, that Grierson would bring a greater precision to their efforts through his highly specialised expertise.

Grierson did two things at the EMB. Firstly, he established a theoretical and critical framework in which the documentary genre could flourish. Secondly, he created an administrative and commercial structure that facilitated the making of these films. Grierson also made sure that the films were seen by circulating the films to schools, film societies, trade unions and various women's organisations.

The EMB also made wide use of newspaper and print media to promote its message. However, it is the posters and films that form its enduring legacy. When the EMB was closed in 1933, Stephen Tallents moved to the General Post Office (GPO) in a move that would be significant for Eckersley-Lombers.

The General Post Office
The modern GPO had grown, from Rowland Hill's initial proposal for pre-paid penny postage in 1837, to become the single largest organisation in Britain. For most of the nineteenth century it had grown and developed organically as new technologies and new systems of organisation were introduced.

For the Post Office, the consequences of the First World War were complex and wide-ranging. In the first instance, the war accelerated the process of mechanisation throughout the service. The scale and complexity of the war effort helped develop new command structures and disciplines that could extend over great distances, and the war also helped introduce new ideas of discipline and responsibility to the workplace. The increasing use of mechanisation was a constant characteristic of the service between about 1920 and 1950, when full operational mechanisation was finally achieved.

The pace of mechanical and administrative modernisation increased the capacity of the service.

Despite these greater capacities, a combination of inflation and economic recession had greatly reduced the profit margins of the postal service and pushed the Post Office into deficit. Suddenly, the convenient arrangements by which the Post Office could raise revenue for the Treasury no longer held.

Accordingly, the Treasury and political administration began to look more closely at issues of efficiency within the Post Office system. The simplest measure of efficiency, in these circumstances, was simply to look at maximising the volumes of service. Having understood the importance of increasing the volumes of service achieved, it was not surprising that the Post Office should attempt to promote its services through the use of public relations and poster publicity.

At the GPO, Tallents simply resolved to continue the good work he had begun at the EMB. A GPO Film Unit was established under John Grierson and a publicity committee was established that added the expertise of Jack Beddington and Kenneth Clark to that of the various GPO representatives.

Tallents established a framework of relations between artist and organisation that gave the artists and designers every opportunity to engage with the great machinery of progress. The first GPO posters were produced as educational resources for schools. Later, posters were displayed in post offices and on GPO vehicles.

Like Frank Pick at the UERL, Stephen Tallents identified a number of themes that needed more or less continuous expression to the public. One such addressed the widespread tendency for people to post letters and parcels at the last minute, which meant a disproportionate volume of work came to the GPO late in the day. This made the effective use of the workforce over the working day more complicated than necessary. By evening out the volumes of traffic across the whole day, the whole system could be made to work more efficiently. Other campaigns promoted the correct parcelling up of packages and the accurate addressing of letters and labels.

The GPO Film Unit continued the work begun at the EMB. Among the films made was Harry Watt and Basil Wright's remarkable story of the night-time travelling post office service between London and Glasgow. The 1936 film, *Night Mail*, incorporated a verse commentary by W.H. Auden and a musical score by Benjamin Britten. Later, the unit produced avant-garde short films by Len Lye and others.

Kenneth Clark, later Lord Clark, had hoped, by helping the GPO, to encourage artists to engage with various aspects of national life and to find a wider range of subjects than the traditional landscape, portrait and still-life. His scheme produced some exciting projects for the GPO. Generally though, the GPO and the artists remained slightly wary of each other. It was only later, in the more urgent and heightened circumstances of the Second World War, that Clark's ideas bore fruit.

Stephen Tallents became Director of Public Relations at the BBC in 1935 and during the Second World War he joined the Ministry of Information.

The advisory committee for publicity at the Post Office records that, on 6 November 1934, a design for a poster had been submitted by Tom Eckersley and Eric Lombers: 'Plan Your Evenings on the Telephone'. The design was rejected. It wasn't until 1938 that the poster 'Visit the Post Office Film Display' began the association between Tom Eckersley, Eric Lombers and the Post Office, a relationship that would last until the 1960s.

Shell-Mex and BP Ltd
Jack Beddington (1893–1959) had been invited to advise the Poster Committee of the GPO in his capacity as publicity manager of Shell-Mex and BP Ltd.

Beddington had come to publicity and public relations almost by accident. He had been rewarded with responsibility for publicity at Shell after expressing forthright criticism of the existing efforts in that domain.

Shell had already, in the course of the 1920s, established themselves as a commercial enterprise with global reach. Their efforts in trading, oil exploration and refining remained mostly hidden from the public, but their presence on garage forecourts and in the rapidly developing world of motoring had made them a familiar name.

Winter Shell
Lorry bill poster, Shell-Mex and BP Ltd,
1938 (with Eric Lombers)
Paul and Karen Rennie collection

The glamour of motoring made it attractive to a wider public. The beginnings of mass-market motoring, during the 1920s, also gave many more people access to the countryside. Cultural conservatives tried to resist the new mechanical phenomenon by resisting the ribbon development and billboard advertising associated with the new road network. It was against this background of conservation that Beddington was invited to develop Shell's publicity and public relations.

Beddington came from a very well-connected family with wide-ranging cultural interests. He was therefore able to direct work towards promising artists and designers.

His instinct was to combine parts of what Frank Pick had achieved at the UERL with those successful elements of what Stephen Tallents had done at the EMB and, later, at the GPO. Beddington began to commission posters and print-media advertising; Eckersley-Lombers produced several posters for Shell during the 1930s. In addition, Shell began to publish motoring guides and to make documentary films.

Austin Reed and Moral Re-Armament

During the 1930s, the menswear manufacturer Austin Reed was at the forefront of the design, manufacturing and marketing of menswear in Britain. The eponymous founder of Austin Reed, in its modern form, had visited America and had seen the enormous potential of consolidation, aggregation and sales to produce profits and to support the emerging consumerist economic model.

The firm had been established during the nineteenth century in Reading. In 1900, the company established a London premises. The firm expanded through a combination of acquisition and output so that by the beginning of the 1920s it had outstripped the capacities of its private backers. In 1920, the firm was recast as a publicly listed company with shares quoted on the London Stock Exchange.

The expansion of London commerce and business administration identified by Austin Reed as the basis for his menswear empire was also part of the process that had provoked Frank Pick to address issues of expansion, integration and co-ordination into a new system of mass transit across London. Austin Reed understood that tidiness and professionalism would be combined in the appearance of this new cadre. The progressive alignment of elements imagined by Austin Reed had also been a characteristic of Frank Pick's holistic and integrated planning at London Transport.

From the start, Austin Reed's aggressive expansion, and its establishment as an anchor of Britain's modern high street, was supported by lively advertising and marketing. The company was among the first to establish proprietary branding, as, for example, applied to its Summit shirt collars.

Austin Reed were already advertising widely at the beginning of the 1920s. In 1929, the firm launched its own menswear magazine, *Modern Man*. The in-house magazine, combining fashion notes and lifestyle choices, provided a new and co-ordinated context for the presentation of Austin Reed as an integrated experience of product and lifestyle.

The advertising and publicity manager for Austin Reed was the writer W.D.H. McCullogh, who was responsible for supervising a roster of artists and designers including Tom Purvis, Edward McKnight Kauffer and Cyril Kenneth Bird (who went by the pen name of Fougasse).

In these circumstances it is not surprising that Austin Reed and Eckersley-Lombers should have sought each other out.

The Reed family were members of the Congregational church, which provided them with a powerful sense of self-determination and Christian revival. Austin Reed himself was a supporter of Frank Buchman's Moral Re-Armament movement, launched in 1938. Moral Re-Armament was just one of a number of groups across Britain that were attempting to square the circle of how to combine the industrial economic system with more humanist and democratic moral structures. The Union for Democratic Control, for example, was a group established in 1914 and active throughout the 1930s that promoted an end to the arms trade and to the militarism associated with economic development.

In 1939 Eckersley-Lombers designed a poster for the Peace Pledge Union. Tom felt what a lot of people felt, that he didn't want another war. People then didn't know what form it might take, and they feared the worst.

In general Eckersley and Lombers were not, at that time, asked to do political posters of the kind associated with the established and militaristic themes of propaganda, although Tom asserted that he would have done so, if it had been something he really believed in. (Speaking much later, he said that he couldn't do a poster for tobacco, although he used to smoke. He felt that it would just be wrong.)

Other Work

There were also opportunities for Eckersley and Lombers in unlikely places that arrived simply by finding a sympathetic spirit. They worked for the *Drapers' Record* and there was a magazine called *Man and His Clothes* at that time. The Nickeloid Electrotype Company was an early patron and afforded the designers a free hand. Eckersley-Lombers also did some illustrations for the newspapers, such as the *News Chronicle*.

Considering the evident success of Eckersley and Lombers in relation to the patronage of London Transport and the GPO described above, it is slightly surprising that they were not so successful in relation to railway advertising. The railway industry had been organised in 1923 into four large regional networks. These were the Southern, the Great Western, the London Midland and Scottish (LMS, operating the west coast), and the London and North Eastern Railway (LNER). A major output of their advertising was aimed at attracting visitors to tourist resorts.

In practical terms, the production of railway posters was organised so that the resort town, railway company, artist and printer each contributed to the process and shared the costs of design, production and display. The resort town would set the brief to promote itself as a holiday or excursion destination. The railway company would co-ordinate artist and printer in relation to the brief and so as to align with its own activities, across its network of services. The resort office would pay the costs of production, and the railway company the costs of display on its own platforms.

The Southern Railway produced relatively few posters beyond those for the seaside resorts it served and for its specialist services to the continent. The Great Western made a signal virtue of its railway heritage, and promoted the South-West as a holiday destination for families. The only real competition between railway companies was that between the LMS and the LNER on the main lines to Scotland.

The Queen magazine cover, 1939 (with Eric Lombers)
Eckersley Archive, LCC

William Teasdale was appointed advertising manager at the LNER in 1923. He was already working at the company and was familiar with the approach of Frank Pick in aligning the visual presentation of messages into something consistent and coherent. In 1926 Teasdale offered exclusive contracts to five of his best-regarded poster designers. The designers were Fred Taylor, Frank Mason, Frank Newbould, Austin Cooper and

Tom Purvis. In the context of the established and formal arrangements between the London and North Eastern and its preferred designers, it was difficult for new designers to gain a foothold.

In contrast, the LMS took a more cautious approach to advertising. They appointed the maritime artist Norman Wilkinson as an advisor to their campaign. Wilkinson was, at this time, already an important and established artist with connections throughout the British art world. He suggested that the LMS should make use of Royal Academicians so as to elevate the quality and status of their posters. He also suggested that the difference between these artistic posters and the more modern offerings elsewhere would help to distinguish the message and the organisation from its rivals.

Another potential market for Eckersley-Lombers was the National Safety First Association, which also commissioned posters to support its campaign for improved road safety awareness and to promote safer working in industrial workshops. It was formed in 1923 and, from the first, used pictorial posters to promote its message. In the 1930s, the NSFA made use of designs by Edward McKnight Kauffer and Hans Schleger for their large billboard posters.

It's slightly surprising that, in this context, the NSFA didn't use Eckersley-Lombers until the very end of the 1930s. The Imperial War Museum have a poster urging everyone to remember to carry their gas masks everywhere.

However, during the course of the Second World War, the NSFA and their successor organisation, the Royal Society for the Prevention of Accidents, would become Tom Eckersley's most important patron.

Teaching

The first classes Tom Eckersley taught were at the Westminster School of Art at an evening class that had been taken originally by the artist Austin Cooper.

One morning in 1937 Eckersley received a telephone call from Cooper to say he was going to be principal of the Reimann School of Commercial and Industrial Art, which was just opening in London. He said he was an admirer of Eckersley's work, and would he like to take over the evening class Cooper was currently teaching?

Cooper, an Anglo-Canadian, as well as being a good teacher was himself a distinguished poster designer and, as mentioned above, was one of five super-poster-designers exclusively contracted to the LNER.

Although the post was relatively short-lived, brought to an end when the school closed at the beginning of the Second World War, Tom Eckersley would go on to teach after the war at the Borough Polytechnic.

Tom Eckersley and Eric Lombers worked in partnership throughout the 1930s and by the end of the decade had had successfully integrated themselves into the relatively small world of British poster design. But the advent of the Second World War caused the partnership to come to an end; despite a brief attempt to revive their working relationship, the paths of the two men diverged after 1945, when Eric Lombers returned north, to Bradford, where he worked at the School of Art.

As well as breaking their partnership and transforming their lives, the war would also revolutionise the practice and processes of design.

London poster project
c. 1936 (with Eric Lombers)
Eckersley Archive, LCC

ALDERSHOT TATTOO

JUNE 11 12 13 16 17 18 19 20

HIRE A BUS FOR YOUR PARTY
HIRE DEPT. 55 BROADWAY S.W.1

Aldershot Tattoo
Panel poster, London Transport, 1936
(with Eric Lombers)
Paul and Karen Rennie collection

London Transport were probably the most significant patrons of modern design in Britain before the Second World War. Indeed, Frank Pick, the organisation's commercial manager, was described by Nikolaus Pevsner as 'the greatest patron'. Panel posters were small images designed to be displayed inside train carriages, buses and ticket-office windows, usually advertising events in and around London. These small-scale posters provided an ideal start in the industry for many young designers.

RUGBY LEAGUE FINAL

WEMBLEY STADIUM APRIL 18 3 P.M.

Stations-Wembley; Wembley Park; Alperton, thence bus 83; or Wembley
Hill or Wembley Stadium (L.N.E.R.)   Buses 18, 18c, 83   Trams 28, 62

Rugby League Final
Panel poster, London Transport, 1936
(with Eric Lombers)
London Transport Museum

BOOK TO MORDEN UNDERGROUND STATION
BUSES EVERY MINUTE · BUS FARE 1'- SINGLE

Epsom Summer Meeting
Panel poster, London Transport, 1938
(with Eric Lombers)
London Transport Museum

England v. Germany
Panel poster, London Transport, 1935
(with Eric Lombers)
London Transport Museum

Wimbledon Championships
Panel poster, London Transport, 1937
(with Eric Lombers)
London Transport Museum

By Bus to the Pictures
Panel poster, London Transport, 1935
(with Eric Lombers)
London Transport Museum

Christmas Shopping for Girls
Panel poster, London Transport, 1936
(with Eric Lombers)
London Transport Museum

Christmas Shopping for Boys
Panel poster, London Transport, 1936
(with Eric Lombers)
London Transport Museum

"The sound of a heavy body falling in the hall. The choking cry of a man in agony."

man in the descended is and went the road. tinkle be- the vehicle,

by P

used to rub- ly with her en. ent. She was happy ghosts, d physical con-

t lined the road irds were sing- till working in sunshine mak- tter. the sound of a clear contralto. e an old man ted forward on wspaper; from ded a wooden

d gave a half- at her as she only his beard d; there were d. is was the last

HEI
LEGA

ECKERSLEY LOMBERS

"When did death occur?"

ECKERSLEY LOMBERS

Editorial illustrations
News Chronicle, 1936 (with Eric Lombers)
Eckersley Archive, LCC

Lorry bill poster, Shell-Mex and
BP Ltd, 1936 (with Eric Lombers)
Paul and Karen Rennie collection

The Shell posters were generally
displayed on the sides of the
flat-bed delivery lorries used
by the company and at their
service stations and garages.
The campaign combined images
of the British landscape with
the slightly more surrealistically
influenced series of conchophile
activities and professions. The
Shell advertising campaign was
managed by Jack Beddington.

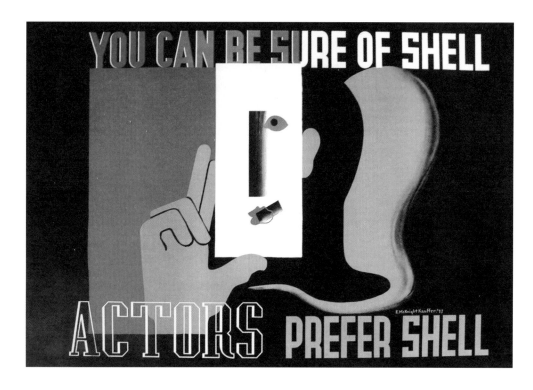

◀ Actors Prefer Shell
Lorry bill poster, Shell-Mex and
BP Ltd, 1936 (with Eric Lombers)
Paul and Karen Rennie collection

▶ Visit the Post Office Film Display
GPO, 1938 (with Eric Lombers)
Paul and Karen Rennie collection

During the 1930s, the GPO used
posters and films to actively
promote its new services to
the wider population. The
documentary films produced by
the GPO Film Unit include the
classic *Night Mail* (1936) with
its combination of poetry, music
and image.

CHAPTER 4

1940s
Crisis and Compatriots

THE **1940s** was a decade in which the experience of the Second World War changed everything in Britain. The war period itself (1939–45) is naturally the more dramatic part of the story, but the remainder of the decade combined economic austerity and a process of rebuilding the country. This rebuilding process extended over the built environment and across the systems and structures of civic life.

From about 1941 onwards, the practical efforts associated with military conflict were extended so as to consider the possible forms of post-war society. The feelings of utopian potential associated with reconstruction were compromised by post-war austerity. Food rationing, for example, had been imposed at the beginning of the war in 1939 and lasted, in part at

least, until 1954. At the same time, British society was transformed by the creation of the welfare state and the provision of modern schools and hospitals.

In this context, and without a specialised design posting within the military establishment, Tom Eckersley was nevertheless able to produce a number of designs both for the war effort and in relation to the home front. His main client during the 1940s was the National Safety First Association (NSFA), which became, in 1941, the Royal Society for the Prevention of Accidents (RoSPA). Eckersley also designed posters for the Ministry of Food and for the General Post Office during this period.

Overall, Eckersley made a remarkable contribution to poster design during the Second World War, perhaps only second in relation to the work of his contemporary Abram Games. Remarkably, Tom Eckersley was able to do this at the same time as being in the RAF. He seems, uniquely, to have found a way to combine his

Telephone Less, GPO, 1945 (detail) Paul and Karen Rennie collection. Full poster shown on page 64.

technical drawing and cartographic duties with working on briefs given him by RoSPA and other organisations. More importantly, his work in the context of the Second World War allowed him to become part of a network of professional colleagues and compatriots working in design in Britain.

In 1938 Eckersley and Lombers had entered a poster design competition for the NSFA. They didn't win a prize but they did get a call from the NSFA's design director, Harry Winbolt, saying how much they had admired the design (and that, actually, they had liked it more than the winner). When Eckersley joined up, he called Winbolt to ask if he could help with any design work. His association with the NSFA and RoSPA began slowly, but lasted in various forms for many years.

The technical nature of machine war required a new kind of optics. It's almost impossible for us, looking back from our twenty-first-century digital realm and with its visual user interface, to understand how few people in 1939 would have been comfortable and familiar with the specialised visual skills required for recognition and interpretation. Even a basic familiarity with maps, plans and wiring diagrams would have been beyond a large part of the population in 1940. Eckersley's professional status would have identified him as a valuable resource within this context of technical conflict.

The RAF

Tom Eckersley joined the Royal Air Force and was first posted to Bedfordshire, where he was an A2 aircraft hand, attached to a drawing office. He would pick up the brief from the NSFA/RoSPA office on one of his day passes and consider the problem while on duty in Bedfordshire. The slightly diminished reliability of the

postal service caused him to work at a reduced scale of half, or quarter-size, of the final poster. One of the things he noticed was that the scaling up of the design produced unexpected changes in texture and grain within the image. These characteristics gave his designs an extra and unexpected dimension.

By now Eckersley was married to Daisy Brown, from Thursby in Cumbria. Soon they had started a family. Anthony Eckersley was born on 20 February 1941. Richard followed and later Paul. Usually, Tom would return home to his wife and sons in Henley-on-Thames, and Daisy would deliver the finished artwork from there.

A colleague in the RAF drawing office had a brother who was in the Intelligence Service in London. In 1943 they contacted Tom and he was posted there, working on maps and in photographic interpretation. The Intelligence Service office contained an interesting group of people, mostly men in their fifties: one had worked in the British Museum, another came from the world of publishing, for instance. There was a different kind of atmosphere from the camp; nobody saluted and it seemed that everyone was in it together. There were four artists in the office, and they did make allowances for the artistic sensibility. While here, Tom Eckersley was promoted to sergeant.

The propaganda demands of war disrupted the cosy relationships between politics, establishment and media. For the most part, the key advertisers and their poster advertisements addressed a metropolitan audience much like themselves. The circumstances of approaching war had made the development of a mass media an urgent priority to support the propaganda efforts required to mobilise the entire population for total war. Accordingly, the print industry and its designers were obliged to embrace the technical possibilities of photo-mechanical offset lithography so as to reduce the make-ready and to speed up the time required to create effective communications.

The beginnings of war, in September 1939, made this shift even more urgent. This shift in technologies had been, in some senses, inevitable. The artistic posters favoured during the 1930s took months to prepare and were expensive in terms of labour and materials. The whole process was dependent on a craft tradition that dated back to the beginnings of industrial lithography in the 1860s.

The relatively few, and very big, lithographic printing companies that controlled the poster-printing business had an effective regional monopoly on plant and craft skills, which had made them reluctant to invest in new machinery and processes. The transition from one type of printing economy to another was marked by the emergence of a new group of printers, equipped with modern machinery.

It is slightly surprising to reflect upon the expansion of the print economy in time of war. Usually, the war economy is presented as circumscribed by shortages. In fact, although there were shortages of paper, materials and people, the sector was encouraged both by government and by a public demand for news and information.

Safety and Industrial Production

The Factories Act of 1937 had established a discretionary duty of care towards workers. This responsibility was addressed, in the first instance, by the National Safety First Association, through the production of simple single-colour posters for workshops. Tom Eckersley's opinion was that, in the main, these poster designs had been unremarkable.

The circumstances of the Second World War made factory safety a much more widely acknowledged priority. The authorities were dismayed to find that, during the early part of the war, the medical resources that had been allocated to treat the victims of enemy aggression were too frequently being claimed by people who had injured themselves in the blackout or in the factory. These accidents were mostly identified as entirely preventable.

For practical purposes, the demands of wartime production linked worker welfare to issues of efficiency and production. For the first time, employers were encouraged to adopt a duty of care to their workers by appeal to patriotic duty. This was especially the case in relation to the large number of new workers drafted into factories and workshops, and as part of the effort to boost production.

In military terms, the beginnings of the war were not a conspicuous success. The British Expeditionary Force in France was forced to make a hasty retreat and abandoned most of its equipment in northern France. On a positive note, the threat of invasion was postponed by the air superiority of the Royal Air Force in the Battle of Britain in 1940. In these circumstances, industrial production became both an economic and military objective of the highest importance, and the evident good sense of an industrial safety campaign was understood and quickly agreed.

In 1940 Winston Churchill had formed an all-party coalition government to run the country during the Second World War and had appointed Ernest Bevin as Minister of Labour. Bevin's experience in the labour movement during the 1920s and 1930s gave him a unique perspective on industrial relations. His vision of the war economy made the alignment between welfare and efficiency explicit. Bevin also understood that welfare gains made during the war were unlikely to be immediately dismantled. He succeeded in maximising the British labour supply, for both the armed services and domestic industrial production, with a minimum of strikes and disruption.

Absenteeism resulting from minor accidents was not just an issue of medical resource; it was also, in the context of war, one of economic and military consequence. The newly named RoSPA addressed these issues through a campaign of simple posters. Ernest Bevin authorised a programme of safety education as part of an effective induction, for inexperienced workers, into the industrial workplace.

The President of RoSPA during the Second World War was Lord Harry McGowan. The role of president was crucial in facing the legislature and guiding the process towards statutory regulation where necessary. Lord McGowan famously declared that 'one of our fighters is missing, if you are off work with an accident.'

McGowan's business career had included the consolidation of the British explosives industry during the First World War and the creation of the ICI industrial conglomerate. Perhaps because of the evident dangers associated with the industrial production of dynamite, McGowan was an important, influential and tireless, advocate of safety at work.

It was noticed that many workers suffered eye injuries as a result of flying debris, splinters and shards within the workshop. These types of injury could very easily, and inexpensively, be reduced by encouraging the wearing of safety goggles.

For the duration of the Second World War, the concerns of accident prevention were aligned with those of the wider war effort, comprising efficiency, morale and production. The alignment of safety messages within the wider framework of public health discourse was an acknowledgement of its significance. Safety campaigns were progressively orientated towards identifying and establishing routines, or patterns, of safety within modern society.

The personalities and expertise of McGowan and Bevin allowed for the strategic alignment of national, industrial and worker interests behind RoSPA's safety campaign.

The demands of industrial production during the Second World War were such that RoSPA's Industrial Service, in its association with the Ministry of Labour, became the largest and most extensive of its services. At the height of this effort, about half a million posters were displayed in factories and workshops around Britain.

The service provided to workshops and factories supplied a combination of graphic posters, illustrational posters and slogan posters. A relatively small selection of posters could be displayed in new combinations and the presentation kept fresh. The posters were supplemented by a series of notes, strip cartoons and educational material for discussion. In addition to all this, factory managers were obliged to provide permanent display areas for poster materials and a dedicated space for safety training.

In order to manage this increased level of activity, it was decided that poster designs should be chosen by panel. The publicity committee, based in London, oversaw the effectiveness of RoSPA's propaganda output. Their terms of reference were to guide and control publicity within the financial constraints specified by the management and finance committees. In addition, they were to control the Society's exhibition policy, to advise on its film policy, to review the work of its operations division, and to report to the executive on all of the above. The committee was also encouraged to adopt a critical position in relation to poster design.

The panel was initially made up of a RoSPA representative and various external experts, and the committee chose posters from open submissions. This process, ad hoc at best, became more systematic with the addition to the panel, during 1941, of Ashley Havinden.

Havinden was a successful and experienced advertising executive and had helped establish the Crawford agency's Berlin office during the 1920s. He had therefore been exposed to the progressive design ideas of the Bauhaus and understood the new design to be both effective and economical. Under Havinden's guidance, the panel gathered together a standing roster of experienced commercial artists and designers who could be called upon to design posters at regular intervals. The panel was further strengthened by the addition of the publisher Francis Meynell.

Meynell was one of the most notable figures in the revival of printing that occurred in Britain between the wars. Together with Oliver Simon and Stanley Morison he was responsible for the extending of an Arts and Crafts sensibility beyond the private press movement and into the mainstream of commercial printing.

Meynell promoted careful printing with machine setting to produce new standards of quality in mass-market printing. His commitment to machine printing was based on the evident economic good sense of machine production. But Meynell also believed that tradition and

Make Sure You Are Seen
RoSPA, 1940s
Paul and Karen Rennie collection

quality could be combined with the machine to produce work that was economic, useful and beautiful.

The association of both Havinden and Meynell with RoSPA gave testimony to its commitment to good design and effective communications. The committee also took an interest in the effective display of their material.

Havinden's contacts within the commercial art environment and his interest in progressive design gave him the chance to promote artists and designers overlooked elsewhere. Among the first names to appear were those of Abram Games, Pat Keely, Tom Eckersley and Eric Lombers. The roster of designers was extended to include the names of the émigré designers Hans Schleger (Zéró), Arnold Rothholz, Manfred Reiss, and those also of Polish designers Jan Le Witt and George Him.

This latter group had established themselves in Europe, and would have been known to Havinden from his days in Berlin and at Crawford's office in London. The creative talent chosen by Havinden and used by RoSPA can be judged as aligned with European modernism in graphic design.

Eckersley's contact with RoSPA also brought him into contact with the designer Leonard Cusden. Cusden was RoSPA's creative director and was instrumental, during the Second World War, in persuading the RoSPA printers, Loxley Brothers of Sheffield, to allow designers to specify the split duct process. This allowed a double colour to be printed with a single pass through the machine. Eckersley became expert in incorporating this effect in his designs. He and Leonard Cusden became firm friends and were later colleagues at the London College of Printing.

Havinden observed that, from the 1920s onwards, he had been impressed by 'the dynamic potential of graphic communication to project effectively'. This was especially true where the prevailing context was one of static and uninspired communication. The factory context of RoSPA's official communications allowed for just such development.

The efforts of Havinden in securing a foothold for modern design thinking is evidence that, whatever the difficulties of the wartime environment, Britain could embrace new ideas. But stylistic experimentation in graphic design would have counted for nothing if it had not also been both economical and effective.

The economics of visual communications, founded on the use of the most up-to-date printing technology and the ruthless simplifications of the design brief, allowed RoSPA to circulate ever-increasing numbers of posters within the industrial community.

Post-war RoSPA

After the war, RoSPA began to re-orientate itself to the changing patterns of civilian life.

The great post-war expansion of motor car ownership was not only about the number of vehicles on the road, it was also about the profile of the typical driver. Car ownership became much more widely spread across the entire population. In consequence, the expression and tone of the messages associated with driving advice had to change. Immediately after the Second World War, RoSPA promoted the idea of road courtesy, especially between drivers and pedestrians, as a way of managing more congested driving environments.

The creation of the National Health Service in 1948 established a climate in which issues of public health became much more widely visible. Tom Eckersley's work for RoSPA during the 1940s was acknowledged as a significant precursor of this sensibility and he received an OBE in 1948 for services to poster design.

In the context of both war and reconstruction, the poster had revealed itself to be effective and economical in shaping public perceptions and behaviour.

The Wartime GPO

The General Post Office was another organisation of crucial strategic significance during the war. As the military scale and complexity of the conflict developed, the public were encouraged to consider the importance of the GPO's services in relation to postal services, telephone communications and savings.

One of the big military ideas of the Second World War was that of combined operations in which the forces of land, sea and air were co-ordinated to achieve a single objective. The planning for these kinds of operations, notably those surrounding the invasion of Europe, quickly outgrew the capacities of the fixed-line, copper wire telephone network, and extended to operational research and scenario planning.

The GPO launched a campaign to remind the public that the use of the telephone should be reserved only for the most important and urgent calls. The finite capacity of the network could, of course, be further compromised by the consequences of enemy action. Once the war was over, of course, another campaign would urge the public to use the telephone more!

As we have seen, Tom Eckersley was already known to the GPO. In 1934, Eckersley and Lombers had submitted an unsolicited design for consideration. That very early design had been rejected, but Eckersley-Lombers were commissioned in 1938 to design a poster for the GPO Film Unit. This commission brought them within the orbit of both Stephen

The World ▲▲▲ at your finger tip

BY OVERSEAS TELEPHONE

By making full use of the Post Office Overseas Telephone Service, you can keep in touch with friends and business associates in every part of the world. This service saves time and worry. A personal conversation will rule out the risk of delay or misunderstanding when you want to send a friendly greeting or an urgent message. Use the overseas telephone and bring the world within call.

Overseas Telephone
Magazine advertising image, GPO, 1940s
Eckersley Archive, LCC

Tallents and Jack Beddington, both important patrons of advertising and graphic design during the 1930s, and now guiding lights of the Ministry of Information during the war, steering the development of design as a form of national projection.

Alexander Highet had been appointed to oversee the GPO's advertising in 1937 as the committee structure of the previous few years began to become less effective. Tom Eckersley remembered Highet as being precise and decisive in his instructions and that, once briefed, he would let the designers get on without interfering. When things did go wrong, he invariably blamed himself for not having briefed the commission accurately. Highet was able to steer the GPO advertising so that it became an expression of national importance.

Eckersley had written to Highet at the GPO from his base in Bedfordshire, and was able to combine his RAF service with producing designs for RoSPA and for the GPO. His first commission from Alexander Highet was 'Address Your Letters Plainly'. Two further posters for the Post Office Savings Bank followed: 'His Action Station' and 'His Needs Come First'.

The Post-war Environment

After the war ended, Eckersley taught at the Borough Polytechnic, where the painter David Bomberg, an admirer of Eckersley's work, was teaching. Rolf Brandt also taught there. Brandt was not an experienced teacher, but he had a wide experience of continental design and photography – his brother was the more illustrious Bill Brandt. Hans Schleger had introduced Rolf to Eckersley, and Rolf showed him his collection of Swiss posters that were unfamiliar to Tom. The two men became friends and would remain colleagues until the 1960s.

The immediate post-war period was a difficult one for graphic designers. The volumes of work associated with the propaganda efforts of the Second World War began to fall away and were only partly replaced by other types of government communications. The advertising industry remained in reduced circumstances for many years while rationing remained in place and the export market was ruthlessly pursued.

As a freelance poster designer, Eckersley found his fair share of clients. He produced posters for the GPO, for London Transport and made a series of posters for Gillette.

Gillette

After the war, Eckersley's posters took a turn towards the whimsical. Looking back he was unable to explain this, except to suggest that, since the economic circumstances immediately after the war were almost worse than during the conflict, a form of wry gallows humour was widespread. He noted the effectiveness of the famous 'Careless Talk' posters by Cyril Bird (Fougasse) that had both sustained morale during the war and reminded everyone to be on their guard.

In A School of Purposes (1946), Bird himself described his design process during the Second World War as combining attraction and persuasion, so as to provoke action. The Fougasse posters were so successful and so well-liked that they provided a form of template for post-war advertising.

The use of humour or wit in advertising and communication design became more widespread in the years after the Second World War and on into the 1950s. (Indeed, a certain lively intelligence was evident in the national celebrations associated with the Festival of Britain, of 1951.)

Good Mornings Begin
with Gillette
Gillette, c. 1948
Paul and Karen Rennie
collection

For Eckersley, and following on in his book illustrations (see below), it was natural to try and integrate a sense of lively humour into his designs for posters. Nowhere was this more evident than in the series of five posters that he designed for Gillette razor blades.

The posters were an elaboration of the masks of the dramatic arts, showing comedy and tragedy; each poster combined a pair of figures or animals with one bearded and frowning and one clean-shaven and smiling. The implied meaning was that, whatever life's ups and downs, things were better with a close shave by Gillette. The pair of figures evoked the idea of our being players upon a stage and made Gillette blades a weapon in the armoury of everyday life. Nowadays, the posters appear slightly confused in their combination of modern illustration juxtaposed with a strapline and image drawn from a much earlier period of Gillette advertising.

Book Illustrating

Eckersley was familiar with the books that had formed part of the fine-press movement in Britain after the First World War. He remembered seeing Arnold Bennett's *Elsie and the Child* (a limited edition, colour-illustrated book with pictures by Edward McKnight Kauffer), for example, while at Salford.

It should come as no surprise that Eckersley should have turned to book illustration as an additional source of income after the Second World War. He drew the pictures for his wife Daisy's book *Cat O'Nine Lives*, published by Peter Lunn in 1946. The work is based around a series of bedtime stories that describe the origin of the famous expression – a cat has nine lives. The resulting adventures are illustrated on coloured papers and with typographic details that conform exactly to the neo-romantic sensibility of the immediate post-war period.

In 1947 Tom drew the pictures for *Animals on Parade* with words by E.A. Cabrelly, published by the Conrad Press, containing large colour illustrations in the tradition of the French educational texts of Père Castor or Kathleen Hale's *Orlando* books.

One of the unexpected features of the 1940s is that, notwithstanding the shortages of paper and ink available to printers and publishers, there was a publishing boom in Britain. *Picture Post* magazine and Penguin paperbacks are probably the best-known elements of this story, but there are many others.

In part, this arose from the same conditions as had supported the alignment between industrial safety, worker welfare and the movement to a post-war settlement that was social democratic in temper. From the beginning of 1941 onwards, various publishers began to produce books and texts that described the possibilities and potential of the British people.

One of the characteristics revealed through media such as George Orwell's writing (*The Lion and the Unicorn*), *Picture Post* magazine ('A Plan for Britain') and Penguin paperback books was that, against all expectations, ordinary British people seemed interested and curious about the world. This was certainly a surprise for the hitherto gentlemanly world of publishing (and politics) which had, during the 1930s, largely and simply addressed itself.

The publishing boom of the Second World War was driven principally by the necessity to communicate with people, and to align their various interests and positions into a social movement that would support the war effort.

The elaboration of titles exploring British values was exemplified by the series of *Britain in Pictures* books. These combined short, essay-type texts with illustrations drawn from the history of British art. After the war, these titles became popular as junior school prizes for academic achievement. The story of these particular books is now relatively well-known. They were conceived as a form of gentle propaganda aimed at the international market, especially ordinary people in the USA.

The publishing boom also gained momentum through the arrival in Britain of refugees from Europe. The circumstances of war in Europe, especially after the arrival of US forces and the successful landings in Normandy, allowed for thoughts to turn in more detailed form to the post-war settlement.

George Weidenfeld, born in Vienna, had arrived in Britain at the end of the 1930s and worked as a journalist during the Second World War. In 1948, he established a publishing firm with Nigel Nicolson to produce a book-magazine hybrid that combined the best parts of the *New Statesman*, *The New Yorker* and *Fortune* magazines. The aim was to combine internationalism, intelligence and comment, across the worlds of politics, business and culture. The publishers called their magazine *Contact*.

Ivor Nicholson and Angus Watson were established publishers that specialised in Nonconformist pamphleteering. They produced *The New Democracy* series of books at the end of the Second World War. These texts, embellished with diagrams by the Isotype Institute and photographs chosen by historian and critic Paul Rotha, explored various social consequences of the Second World War, such as the impact of women on the world of work. The Isotype system provided a pictorial language for the communication of statistical information to ordinary people. The Institute was established in Vienna by Otto Neurath and his wife Olga Hahn-Neurath. Isotype presentation was popular in the late 1930s and especially during the 1940s as an element in the graphic presentation of post-war reconstruction.

Against this background of heightened activity, it is not that surprising that Tom Eckersley should have found a number of opportunities within publishing after the war.

Ealing Films

Nowadays, the Ealing productions of the 1940s and 1950s are recognised as forming a body of work comprising reassuring war dramas and a series of lively and charming comedies.

In general, the film poster is something that has to combine a number of different elements: a visual sense of the theme of the story, along with the title and all the production credits. Typically, this has resulted in designs that are congested. In graphic design, congestion is usually not a good thing and results in sense of confusion and illegibility. In consequence, a lot of film posters are, whatever their merits, diminished from the point of view of design.

The advertising director of Ealing Studios was S. John Woods. Woods was a designer, typographer and artist himself. Upon his appointment he resolved to build upon the ideas of his predecessor in the role, the Russian Monja Danischewsky, and to promote the Ealing films with first-rate posters by first-rate artists and designers. Woods assembled an impressive line-up of artists, and carefully matched artist and film for each project.

The comedy *Whisky Galore!* (1949) tells the story of a local uprising, a typical theme for an Ealing comedy. The people of a remote Scottish island conspire to outfox the forces of unsympathetic, distant and dour administration so as to salvage a large quantity of whisky from the wreck of a coastal freighter.

Tom Eckersley was invited by Woods to design the poster for the film. His design combines elements of typography and photography, framed within a dynamic and lively rendering of a whisky bottle against the island backdrop. The rosy-cheeked face on the bottle was probably enough to convince cinemagoers of the likely outcome of the escapade.

Whisky Galore film poster
1949
Ealing Studios/Album/Alamy

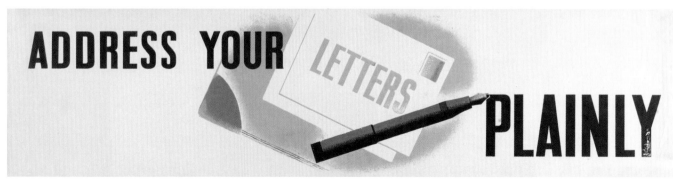

◀ Telephone Less
GPO, 1945
Paul and Karen Rennie collection

During the Second World War, the
telephone communication network
of copper wires had, as much as
possible, to remain free for use
by the military authorities. The
Post Office produced posters to
encourage a more considered use
of the telephone. After the war,
a similar campaign was begun to
encourage telephone communication
once again.

▶ Take Your Gas Mask Everywhere
RoSPA, 1939
Paul and Karen Rennie collection

◀ Address Letters Plainly
GPO, c. 1944
Eckersley Archive, LCC

TAKE YOUR GAS MASK EVERYWHERE

ECKERSLEY-LOMBERS.39

Issued jointly by The National Safety First Association (Inc.), Terminal House, 52, Grosvenor Gardens, London, S.W.1, and The Industrial Welfare Society (Inc.), 14 Hobart Place, London, S.W.1.
ARP/1
LOXLEY BROTHERS LTD, LONDON & SHEFFIELD.

His Needs Come First
GPO, 1944
Paul and Karen Rennie collection,
ex Herbert Robinson

The important role of the GPO during the Second World War is not as widely acknowledged as it should be. The Post Office played a significant role in maintaining normal communications in extraordinary times. As well as providing savings accounts and its many usual services, it played a crucial role in the development of the electronic machinery that supported the code-breaking at Bletchley Park.

HIS ACTION STATION

SAVING IS EVERYBODY'S WAR JOB POST OFFICE SAVINGS BANK

Eckersley. 43

His Action Station
GPO, 1943
Paul and Karen Rennie collection,
ex Herbert Robinson

THOUSANDS HAVE ALREADY JOINED   HOW ABOUT YOU ?

JOIN THE REGULAR AIR FORCE

Join the Regular Air Force
RAF, 1946
Paul and Karen Rennie collection

After the Second World War, Tom
Eckersley produced a number of
posters for the Royal Air Force.
These posters are notable for their
use of photo-montage, made possible
by developments in photo-mechanical
reproduction.

UNIFORMS BY AUSTIN REED

Uniforms by Austin Reed
Austin Reed, 1940
Eckersley Archive, LCC

Austin Reed was one of a number
of menswear and tailoring firms that
produced bespoke uniforms for the
officer classes during the Second
World War.

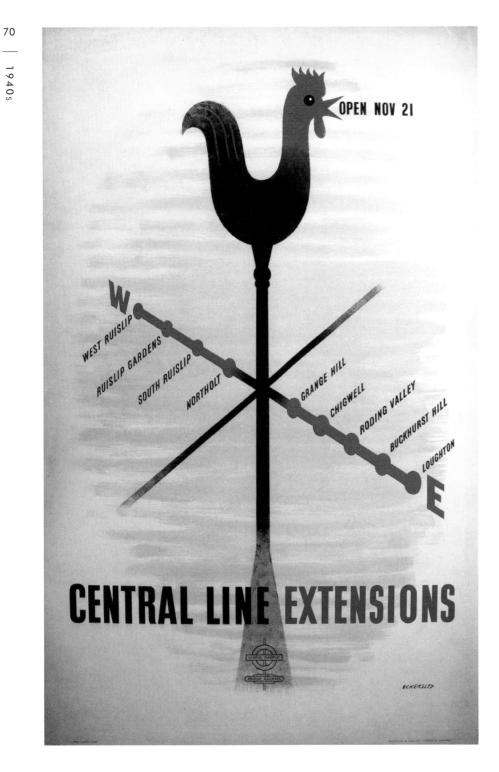

Exact Fare
London Transport, 1944
Eckersley Archive, LCC

ON TRAINS · BUSES · TRAMS
APPLY LOST PROPERTY OFFICE
200 BAKER STREET N.W.1
Open Monday to Friday 10 to 6   Saturday 10 to 1

★ Adjoining Baker Street Station

Lost Property
London Transport, 1944
Eckersley Archive, LCC

KLM Royal Dutch Airlines, 1948
Eckersley Archive, LCC

Broken Strands
RoSPA, 1943
Paul and Karen Rennie Collection

The advent of the Second World War quickly identified the problem of safety as one aligned with the urgent requirements of war production and general efficiency. RoSPA's industrial safety propaganda was co-opted into the Ministry of Labour for the duration. RoSPA made use of many designers, including Tom Eckersley, to produce posters.

Stow Tools Safely
RoSPA, 1942
Paul and Karen Rennie Collection

Take the Right Steps
RoSPA, 1943
Paul and Karen Rennie Collection

Broken Rungs Cause Broken Limbs
RoSPA, 1944
Paul and Karen Rennie Collection

Take Warning Wear Goggles
RoSPA, 1942
Paul and Karen Rennie Collection

REPORT DEFECTS

Issued by the Royal Society for the Prevention of Accidents, Terminal House, 52 Grosvenor Gardens, London, S.W.1.

Report Defects
RoSPA, 1946
Paul and Karen Rennie Collection

Rogues Gallery No. 2
RoSPA, 1945
Paul and Karen Rennie Collection

Inspect Daily
RoSPA, 1943
Paul and Karen Rennie Collection

Replace Covers, Prevent Falls
RoSPA, 1941
Paul and Karen Rennie Collection

Asking for Trouble
RoSPA, 1941
Paul and Karen Rennie Collection

◀◀ Stack Safely
RoSPA, 1944
Paul and Karen Rennie
Collection

◀ Stand From Under
RoSPA, 1944
Paul and Karen Rennie
Collection

Handtraps
RoSPA, 1946
Paul and Karen Rennie Collection

The process of split duct printing
allowed for two colours to be printed
by one pass through the machine.
This effectively allowed a two-colour
machine to print a four-colour design.
The technical staff at Loxley Brothers,
where the RoSPA posters were printed,
were adept at the precise machine-
minding required for this.

SOUND TOOLS-SAFER WORKING

Sound Tools – Safer Working
RoSPA, 1947
Paul and Karen Rennie Collection

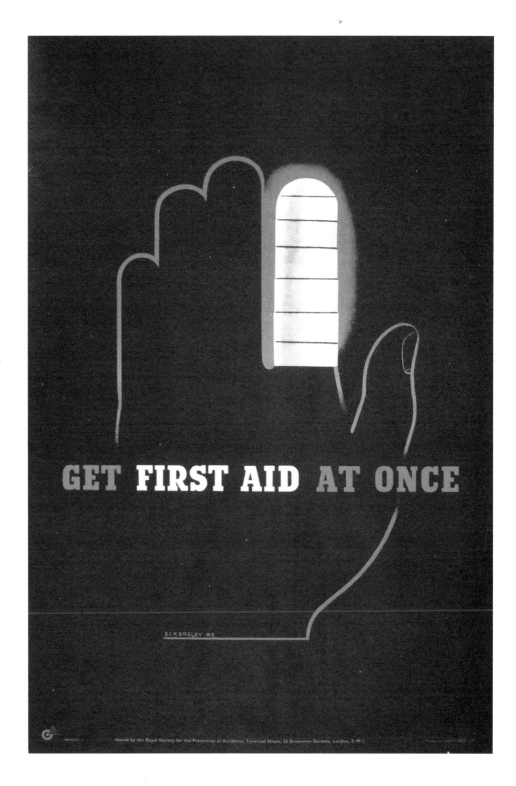

Get First Aid At Once
RoSPA, 1948
Paul and Karen Rennie Collection

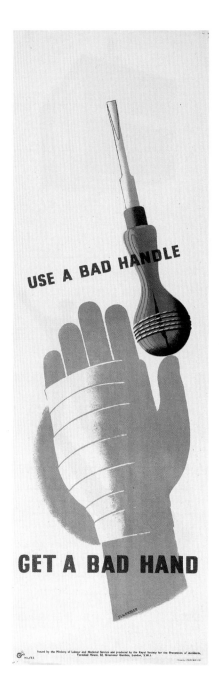

Roll Them Up
RoSPA, 1942
Eckersley Archive, LCC

Bad Handle, Bad Hand
RoSPA, 1942
Eckersley Archive, LCC

Not to Return to Work
RoSPA, 1942
Eckersley Archive, LCC

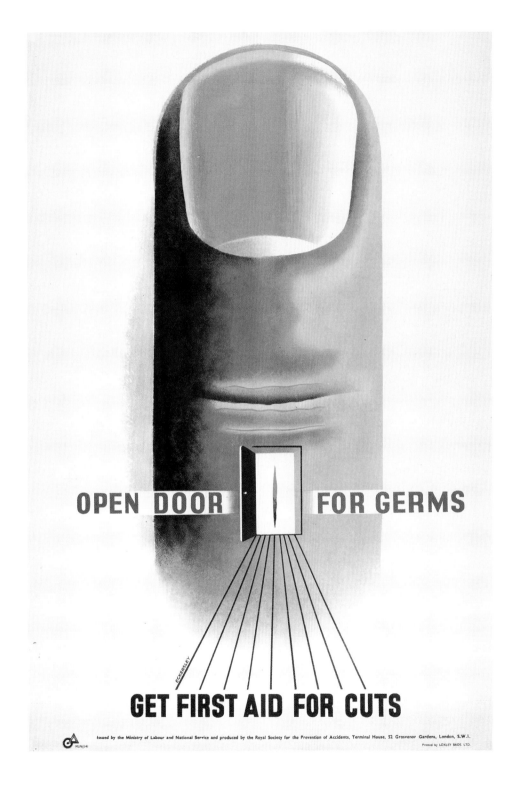

OPEN DOOR ▮ **FOR GERMS**

GET FIRST AID FOR CUTS

Issued by the Ministry of Labour and National Service and produced by the Royal Society for the Prevention of Accidents, Terminal House, 52 Grosvenor Gardens, London, S.W.I.

Printed by LOXLEY BROS. LTD.

Open Door for Germs
RoSPA, 1943
Eckersley Archive, LCC

Wipe it Up
RoSPA, 1943
Eckersley Archive, LCC

Green Vegetables
Ministry of Food, 1942
(with Eric Lombers)
Paul and Karen Rennie Collection

At the end of the Second World War,
the design partnership between Tom
Eckersley and Eric Lombers was briefly
re-established. The difficulties of the
post-war economy combined with
the additional responsibilities of
family life made the collaboration
impossible to sustain.

Children About?
RoSPA, 1950
Paul and Karen Rennie collection

A Child's Life
RoSPA, 1950s
Paul and Karen Rennie collection

You Are Being Followed
RoSPA, 1948
Paul and Karen Rennie collection

A Happy Christmas
RoSPA, 1950
Paul and Karen Rennie collection

A Safe Holiday
RoSPA, 1948
Paul and Karen Rennie collection

motorists observe

pedestrians use

the proper crossings

T.Eckersley '46
E.Lombers

Issued by the Royal Society for the Prevention of Accidents, Terminal House, 52, Grosvenor Gardens, London, S.W.1

Printed by LOXLEY BROS. LTD.

Motorists Observe
RoSPA, 1946 (with Eric Lombers)
Paul and Karen Rennie collection

You Bought Him a Bicycle
RoSPA, 1944
Eckersley Archive, LCC

Eno's Fruit Salt, 1947
Eckersley Archive, LCC

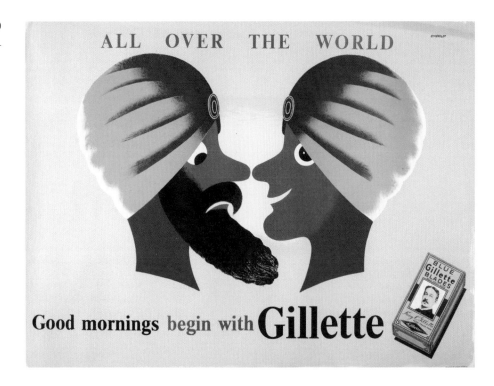

All Over the World
Gillette, 1948
Eckersley Archive, LCC

Good Mornings Begin with Gillette
Gillette, 1948
Eckersley Archive, LCC

Sailor
Seven Seas, 1948
Paul and Karen Rennie collection

Neptune
Seven Seas, 1948
Eckersley Archive, LCC

ANIMALS ON PARADE

ILLUSTRATIONS BY ECKERSLEY   WORDS BY E. A. CABRELLY

◁ *Animals on Parade* by
E.A. Cabrelly, book jacket
illustration
The Conrad Press, 1947
Eckersley Archive, LCC

▷ Lion illustration from
Animals on Parade
The Conrad Press, 1947
Eckersley Archive, LCC

One of the unexpected
characteristics of the Home
Front during the Second
World War is that, paper
shortages notwithstanding,
the war provided a boom for
the print economy. This was
especially true in relation to
illustrated children's books,
and it is within this context
that Tom Eckersley produced
his two illustrated books.

◀ Illustration from *Cat O'Nine Lives*
by Daisy Eckersley
Peter Lunn, 1946
Eckersley Archive, LCC

▶ Dog illustration from
Animals on Parade
The Conrad Press, 1947
Eckersley Archive, LCC

CHAPTER 5

1950s

International Colleagues and Outlook

THE 1950s was a decade in which the design profession began to consolidate across both Europe and North America. It did so, in these different contexts, in slightly different ways. In Europe, the background of post-war reconstruction provided an environment that, in the short term, redirected resources away from communication and towards the practicalities of building and export. I don't mean that the design industry consolidated through the traditional activity of mergers and acquisitions, but that the various practitioners, so individually isolated during the 1940s, began to network more effectively. Together, they became more than the sum of their parts. In part, this was an entirely pragmatic response to the continuous difficulties of working independently.

Colour magazine advertising (detail)
British Aluminium Co., 1950s
Eckersley Archive, LCC. Full advert on page 119.

Eckersley remembered the 1950s as a difficult time in his career, which he sustained by combining his poster design with teaching posts at Borough Polytechnic and, later, the London College of Printing. Throughout the 1950s and 1960s, he continued to design posters for London Transport and for the GPO.

The Festival of Britain in 1951 established a template for the integration of architecture, art and design into a coherent and material expression of post-war optimism. Eckersley entered the competition to design the symbol for the Festival but was unsuccessful against the jaunty 'Britannia with bunting' design by Abram Games. The list of designs for consideration had also included efforts by Robin Day, Milner Gray and F.H.K. Henrion.

This group, along with Hans Schleger (Zéró), effectively transformed the role of designer in mid-century Britain. Eckersley's inclusion among this group recognised his position at the very top of graphic design in Britain at that time.

In 1952 he was chosen, along with these contemporaries, as a representative of British graphic design as part of a British Council Exhibition to Stockholm and Scandinavia. The designers included in the exhibition were Tom Eckersley, Abram Games, Ashley Havinden, F.H.K. Henrion, Pat Keely, Hans Schleger, Jan Le Witt and George Him. In practical terms, these were the outward-facing and internationalist British designers associated with the Alliance Graphique Internationale.

Alliance Graphique Internationale

The origins of the AGI were Franco-Swiss and marked a European attempt to develop an international community of design in the graphic arts. The name Alliance Graphique had first been used at the beginning of the 1930s by Cassandre and Charles Loupot for their creative agency in Paris.

The new post-war Alliance Graphique began informally as a consequence of the important poster exhibition organised by Paul Colin in 1948 under the title 'Exposition de l'Affiche Française'.

A number of European designers who had made their names before the war were curious to find out about their erstwhile friends and colleagues. The displacements and upheavals of the conflict had broken whatever network had existed previously. The association began with a tentative meeting between French and Swiss designers brokered by the publisher Alfred Girardelos. At his suggestion, the Swiss illustrator and designer Heiri Steiner contacted a number of colleagues: Donald Brun and Fritz Buhler from Switzerland, and Jean Colin, Jean Picart le Doux and Jacques Nathan Garamond from France.

The association was established as a very informal affair, its objective being simply to encourage the best-known designers from various countries to meet and exchange ideas through convivial interaction, often involving restaurants and cocktail parties. In 1951, it was established on a more formal footing from its base in Paris.

The first executive comprised Le Doux as president, Buhler as vice president, Garamond as treasurer and Jean Colin the secretary. The first AGM was held in Paris during 1951.

Membership was by invitation only. The group was extended by adding to the founding group other designers from France and Switzerland. A little later, designers from Great Britain were added. Tom Eckersley, Barnett Freedman, Milner Gray, Ashley Havinden, F.H.K. Henrion, Jan Le Witt and George Him were all elected members. Abram Games refused the invitation. The second AGM was held in London during 1952. In practical terms, and for designers working in Britain, the AGI consolidated the 'community of practice' identified by Ashley Havinden within the context of the 1940s RoSPA campaign.

In 1955, the AGI organised a more ambitious and public-facing exhibition at the Louvre, Paris. In his introductory essay to the exhibition, Jean Carlu wrote: 'The first exhibition of the AGI is not merely a remarkable collection of graphic work from all corners of the earth. It is first and foremost an expression of affinity ...'

There were other important exhibitions of posters and graphic design in the 1950s, notably London in 1956 and Lausanne in 1958.

Eckersley was already familiar to his continental colleagues through various publications. He had first featured in 1946 when included in the overview of British design in issue number 14 of the Swiss graphic design magazine *Graphis*. In 1950, he was invited to design the cover of *Graphis*, issue number 31. This was a rare honour. His work was also included in that issue's survey of British commercial art. Then, in 1954, the magazine published an illustrated article about Eckersley and his work.

Graphis magazine was established in Switzerland during 1944. It provided an international and independent view about developments in graphic design and communication and was clearly intended to position itself in readiness for the opportunities and challenges of post-war reconstruction.

Graphis was by no means the first design magazine. There had been various efforts to establish specialised design publications in Britain and France during the 1930s. In Britain, *Commercial Art* and *Studio Publications* were probably the most widely known. At the end of the 1930s, the Shenval Press published *Typography*, a title that reflected the increased significance of typographic consideration in modern printing and design. *Typography* lasted eight issues. Later, the Shenval Press published equally short-lived but influential magazines, *Alphabet* and *Alphabet and Image*. In France, *Les Arts et Métiers Graphiques* was the stand-out magazine publication of the inter-war years.

The longest established poster and graphic design magazine was the German *Gebrauchsgraphik*, founded in 1924 by Professor H.K. Frenzel. The magazine relaunched after the Second World War, and in the February

Graphis No. 31 magazine cover, Switzerland, 1950
Eckersley Archive, LCC

1950 issue they included a pictorial survey of RoSPA's accident prevention posters in which several Eckersley designs were included. It is certainly the case that, in the early 1950s, Tom Eckersley was one of the few British graphic artists and poster designers with an international reputation.

The AGI exhibitions were a pan-European attempt to offer an alternative vision of graphic design to that prevailing in the USA and represented by the annual design conference at Aspen that had begun in 1949. The link between applied art and industry taught at the Bauhaus had successfully been transferred to North America as part of a trajectory of modernist ideas that linked Moscow, Berlin, Paris and New York. The alignment between modernist values and consumer capitalism was, in North America, taken as a given. In Europe an opportunity existed, within the context of reconstruction, for design to align itself with a form of social progress.

Tom Eckersley maintained his links with the AGI throughout the 1950s and 1960s. He often appears in the background of photographs as a dapper, slightly removed personality with moustache, suit and cigarette.

Like many designers Eckersley produced his own Christmas cards and exchanged them with his friends and colleagues in Britain and Europe. He was always especially pleased to receive cards from his colleagues at the AGI.

Poster Design, 1954

The AGI gave Tom Eckersley an opportunity to share ideas from across Europe and to become aware of international developments in graphic design and poster art. The internationalism of his outlook was reflected in the choice of posters he made to illustrate his book *Poster Design*, published in 1954.

The book was part of an extensive series on different aspects of creative practice, which provided simple instructions for students and enthusiasts. The books were a staple of art education in the 1950s.

Before the Second World War art education had been, more or less, of the fine art or commercial and trade variety. The outlook was certainly insular, if not parochial. Post-war developments focused on developing specific skills for a market defined by rapidly changing technologies and material science. Furthermore, the future success of British industry was dependent on both a home market of consumer products aimed at a widening segment of society and an international export market. By the time of the 1956 AGI exhibition in London, it was clear that graphic design, communication and advertising would all have substantial contributions to make to that project.

As always, Eckersley gave uncomplicated and practical advice. He eschewed most poster history, on the basis that this was covered elsewhere, and focused on drawing attention to striking examples of contemporary poster design. The index of posters included in the book show Tom drawing examples by reference to the work of his international colleagues in the AGI.

The Design Research Unit and Mass Observation

The British military experience of the Second World War was defined, in the main, as combined operations. This involved the close collaboration with allies and the consideration of problems and objectives in the round.

It wasn't surprising that this approach should transfer to the equally daunting post-war challenges associated with rebooting the economy and rebuilding.

In design terms, this experience provided a template for the multi-disciplinary studio, although it took a while for this model to emerge in a commercially sustainable form. After 1945, and the Festival of Britain notwithstanding, creative opportunities became much more limited. The Design Research Unit (DRU) had been founded in 1943 as the exemplar of the multi-disciplinary agency that could provide services at the scale and speed required of government.

The DRU was formed by Marcus Brumwell, the managing director of Stuart's Advertising, and by Herbert Read. Marcus Brumwell was an advertising pioneer, arts patron and political activist. Nowadays, he is probably best known as the early patron of the British modern architects Team 4, comprising Richard Rogers and Su Rogers (née Brumwell – Marcus's daughter), Norman Foster and Wendy Cheesman.

Herbert Read was a writer and intellectual who was the most significant figure in British arts culture during the middle part of the twentieth century. He was an early advocate of surrealism and its associated characteristics of humanistic therapeutic and psychological benefit, and a tireless advocate of the benefits of art for everyone, regardless of class or background. In 1946, Lund Humphries published a collection of essays describing the practice of design in the context of a modernist rebuilding of Britain. Herbert Read wrote the introduction. Seven of the contributors were members of the DRU.

The combination of the flamboyant and business-savvy Brumwell and the intellectual Read provided a compelling and convincing entry, for the DRU, into the world of politics and administration. Indeed, Brumwell's aim was to leverage the accelerated technological development associated with war, and to apply it to the social sphere. Brumwell was notorious for his deployment of the sartorial signifiers of creative eccentricity and moral seriousness – bright ties, pressed shirts and serious glasses.

Quite apart from the individual artists and designers associated with the DRU, the organisation gave shape to an emerging philosophy of design and reconstruction and applied it to outcomes in 3D, graphics, exhibitions and architecture and industrial design. The roll call of personalities associated with the DRU included Misha Black, Milner Gray and Kenneth Bayes.

The provision of services provided by the DRU and its guiding philosophy could be transformed and substantiated by appeal to market-research data and to the stories collected through Mass Observation (MO).

The Mass Observation movement had been founded in the 1930s by Tom Harrisson, Charles Madge and Humphrey Jennings. MO was founded on the basis that the democratic extensions that followed the First World War would require the institutions of government to extend their understanding of these new constituencies. In order to facilitate this, MO began to collect testimony and stories of lived experience from sources around the UK and especially in the industrial North. From the first, MO augmented this material with documentary photographs, by Humphrey Spender for example, and documentary films by Humphrey Jennings. This kind of material gave visual form to the photographic weekly news magazine *Picture Post*, founded in 1938.

Through the personality and energy of Marcus Brumwell, the DRU promoted the activities of design as a philosophical project of reconstruction and progress. The explicit association, within the methodology of MO, between scientific quantitative data collection and the expression of feeling was described as 'the science of ourselves'. The methodology combined the progressive aspects of machine philosophy, design reform, scientific management and operational research.

Artist Partners

Against the background of freelance uncertainty and economic austerity of the early 1950s, Eckersley joined the creative agency Artist Partners. The agency provided commercial representation and administrative services to artists and creative designers, allowing them to focus and concentrate on the process and work they enjoyed. Eckersley had already been featured in *Designers in Britain* and was a member of the AGI. Artist Partners cemented this international recognition and gave it a commercial focus.

The association gave Tom commercial representation on an international stage. Artist Partners were mostly illustration-based, an emphasis that reflected the reality of publishing, magazine and advertising art during the 1950s.

The agency was formed in 1951 by Don Candler and John Barker, along with L.A. Rix, Betty Luton White and the designer Reginald Mount. The agency quickly expanded its representation to include specialist categories such as fashion and sophistication, humour and creative design.

From the start the agency took an internationalist view and represented partners from France, continental Europe and North America, such as André François, Jean Colin, Savignac and Saul Bass among many more.

The agency also cultivated a cosmopolitan style, derived from the example of Brumwell and the DRU. After relocating to Mayfair's Dover Street, the Partners held regular parties at which creatives and clients could mix. This was a very different way of working from the cramped rooms of Eckersley-Lombers in Ebury Street back in the 1930s.

Artist Partners published spiral-bound catalogues of work for circulation to clients. Tom Eckersley is included in the first and second catalogues, from 1954 and 1958, listed under 'creative design'. The catalogues show a double-page spread of examples of work in poster design and cover designs.

The company also had a print finishing workshop and, even in 1954, were promoting silk-screen printing as an economic process for short-run and point-of-sale material. The development of brighter inks also gave silk screen a contemporary look that made it suitable for the developing consumer economy in Britain.

In 1957, Tom designed the Lion safety mark for the Egg Marketing Board. This mark was then printed on every egg produced in Britain as an indicator of safety and quality.

London College of Printing (LCP), Back Hill

In 1954 Tom Eckersley was invited to join the staff at the London School of Printing and Graphic Arts (renamed in 1962 the London College of Printing). The college was mindful of the need to expand its activities and to place itself at the forefront of the technical developments noted above, and to better understand the cultural ramifications of these changes.

Eckersley had received a call from Bill Stobbs, who was Head of Design at LCP. Stobbs was well-known as a book illustrator. He advised Eckersley that there was a job he should apply for. The prospect of a full-time teaching post was something he had never considered before, although the uncertainties of freelance activity made the opportunity sound attractive.

Stobbs convinced Eckersley with the assurance that he would be able to combine the teaching with his own practice. Tom recalled that, by a strange quirk, demand for his work picked up at just the time that he accepted the job. But he never regretted his decision to join LCP.

Stobbs and Eckersley proved a good team. Stobbs was an able administrator and allowed Eckersley to focus on the creative management of the course. Eckersley arranged exhibitions, like the ones he had seen as a student in Salford, of work by interesting international designers such as Saul Bass and Paul Rand. The school looked beyond its immediate local environment and adopted a more expansive outlook in relation to design and its objects.

Eckersley, in common with many poster artists of the 1930s, had begun his career in an era of hand-drawn lettering. By the 1950s typography had developed so as to become the foundation for graphic design practice, in part because of the accuracy of its technical specification. His arrival at LCP gave him access to colleagues with greater practical experience in typography and lettering as part of poster design.

Bill Stobbs moved to Maidstone School of Art in 1957 and Tom Eckersley was promoted to take his place as the LCP's Head of Design.

The historical development of the London College of Printing and Graphic Arts had begun as the London trade school of the printing industry. The beginnings of the College were, unsurprisingly, near Fleet Street, where evening classes were made available to the young apprentices of the newspaper and printing industries through St Bride's Institute and the Bolt Court Technical School at the end of the nineteenth century. The St Bride's Institute eventually took on larger premises in Stamford Street, Blackfriars, where it was renamed the London School of Printing.

By 1943, it was clear that the school would require new facilities. Partly, this was due to the depredations of war, but also to the emerging political consensus that Britain's post-war society would be driven by scientific and technological change. Information and communication design would provide a significant and powerful support for this social, technological and economic development.

In 1949 the London County Council incorporated Bolt Court into the main School of Printing. Some courses from Stamford Street and Bolt Court were moved to a single building at Back Hill, Farringdon, which afforded space for expansion.

The first incarnation of the Design School had premises at Back Hill, where Tom Eckersley was invited to direct the activities of the school. Eckersley had been a member of the small, but significant, group of graphic designers that had effectively transformed the print environment in Britain during, and after, the Second World War. Through their efforts the term 'commercial art' had been replaced by 'graphic design' (the formal arrangement of image and type) and by illustration and photography. Now, Eckersley became part of a second influential group that transformed design education in readiness for what would happen in the 1960s and later.

poster design

ECKERSLEY

the Studio 'how to do it' series · 50

*How to Do It: Poster
Design* book cover and
interior image
The Studio, 1954
Paul and Karen Rennie
collection

The *How to Do It* series
of books, published by
The Studio, provided
simple advice for art
students. The series
comprised a large
range of titles and
covered many aspects
of art and design.

In more extended form, this group also included Misha Black, Ashley Havinden, Robin Day and Terence Conran. Though not graphic designers, each were instrumental in these wider transformations of style and taste.

The building at Back Hill has a deep light well, or atrium, at its centre and the floor plans were arranged as corridors with workshops, offices and studios at intervals around the external circumference of the structure. The building also housed the photographic departments and a canteen area for staff and students. This environment offered a rich potential for useful interaction.

The proximity of design and photographic activities also accelerated a process of integrating photographic process into graphic design. The new work distinguished itself from the prevailing illustrational norm of commercial art at the time, and identified itself as sophisticated and contemporary-looking. This made the work attractive to the developing consumer economy.

The development of economic photo-mechanical processes, begun during the 1930s, had accelerated during the Second World War and continued into the 1950s. The craft skills of stone-based colour lithography disappeared and were replaced by a single four-colour photo-offset process, and the process of design became increasingly one of technocratic specification.

It also became possible, particularly with silk screen, to produce short-run designs relatively cheaply in new and exciting contemporary colours. These opportunities continued to expand rapidly during the 1960s with a demand fuelled by youthful counterculturalism. The pop posters of the psychedelic movement made full use of this technical potential and addressed a market of student bedsits and campus residencies. By the end of the 1950s it was obvious to Eckersley that commercial art would be unable to deliver the wide range of outcomes and services required by a rapidly changing consumer society.

In a far-sighted move, the team at Back Hill began to think about how best to prepare students for an activity that, in 1957, didn't really yet exist! The exact origins of the term 'graphic design' remain contentious. It is unclear exactly when the term was first used, and by whom, in Britain.

The graphic designer Richard Hollis was a colleague of Eckersley's at Back Hill. He recalls that students responded positively to the eclectic range of tutors assembled as a team around Eckersley. Former student David King recalls that there was a real sense, some fifteen years after the end of the Second World War, of wanting to produce something new and exciting, even if you weren't quite sure what it would look like. The open-mindedness of Tom Eckersley translated itself into a course team and environment that supported the creation of individual work as a consequence of a specific intellectual and practical approach to design. It certainly wasn't about creating another generation in the style of Eckersley, or anyone else.

Hollis, who was not much older than the students themselves at the time, had through previous experience as both student and teacher learned about letterpress printing, lithography and silk-screen printing. He was therefore perfectly qualified to introduce the students to these distinct practices and to show them how to combine image-making with careful and precise typographic consideration.

Tom Eckersley's team-building also brought together kindred spirits. Hollis found himself part of a group of sympathetic colleagues which included Robin Fior. Hollis and Fior found common cause, along with Ken Garland, working on posters for the nascent counterculture of protest, and as associates of the Campaign for Nuclear Disarmament and its marches from Aldermaston.

The environment at Back Hill fostered exactly the kinds of collaboration, with typography at its core, that came to define the term 'graphic design'.

It was still possible, at the end of the 1950s, for Eckersley to draw on friends and colleagues from the pre-war and immediate post-war period to staff the department. George Adams arrived, who had been a student at the Bauhaus under his former name of Georg Teltcher. Rolf Brandt, brother of photographer Bill, was another link with the original émigré sources of modernism. Rolf's approach, as an illustrator in commercial design, was less formally austere than the modernist orthodoxy of the 1920s. Eckersley's achievement at Back Hill was to begin developing the elements of a visual language for post-war Britain.

ECKERSLEY

Aluminium   reduces tyre wear

The BRITISH ALUMINIUM Co Ltd

NORFOLK HOUSE   ST JAMES'S SQUARE   LONDON SW1

Colour magazine
advertising
British Aluminium Co.,
1950s
Eckersley Archive, LCC

ECKERSLEY

Aluminium increases carrying capacity

The BRITISH ALUMINIUM Co Ltd

NORFOLK HOUSE ST JAMES'S SQUARE LONDON SW1

Colour magazine
advertising
British Aluminium Co.,
1950s
Eckersley Archive, LCC

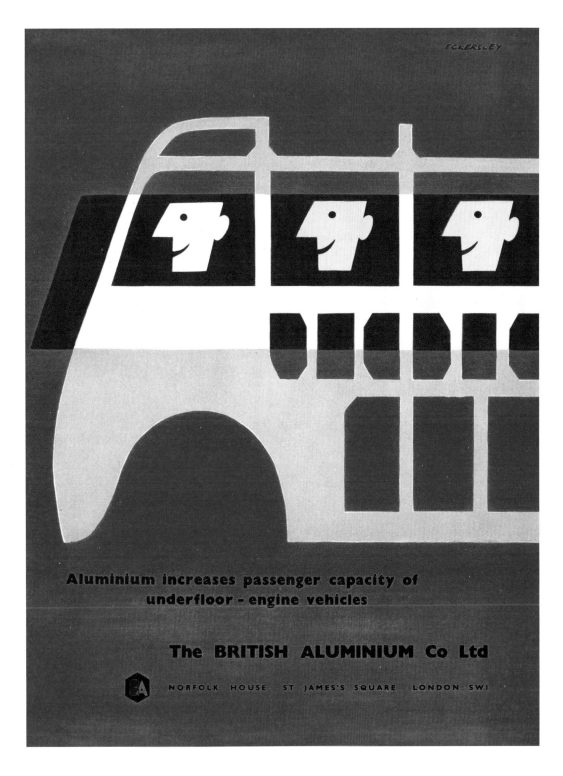

Colour magazine
advertising
British Aluminium Co.,
1950s
Eckersley Archive, LCC

Aluminium increases payload

The BRITISH ALUMINIUM Co Ltd

NORFOLK HOUSE ST JAMES'S SQUARE LONDON SW1

Colour magazine
advertising
British Aluminium Co.,
1950s
Eckersley Archive, LCC

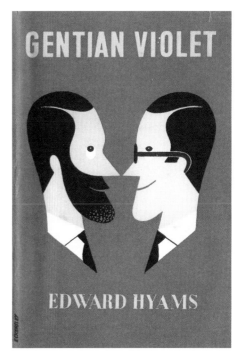

▲ **Books on Sport point-of-sale showcard**
1950s
Eckersley Archive, LCC

▶ *Gentian Violet* **by Edward Hyams**
Book cover, Longmans, Green and Co.,
1953
Eckersley Archive, LCC

Top People of Tomorrow Take *The Times* Today
The Times newspaper, 1959
Eckersley Archive, LCC

Top People Take *The Times*
The Times newspaper, 1959
Eckersley Archive, LCC

Sales Appeal
Magazine cover, 1952
Eckersley Archive, LCC

Sales Appeal
Magazine cover, 1952
Eckersley Archive, LCC

Begin Saving for Me
Post Office Savings Bank, 1950s
Eckersley Archive, LCC

For Growing Needs …
Post Office Savings Bank, 1950s
Eckersley Archive, LCC

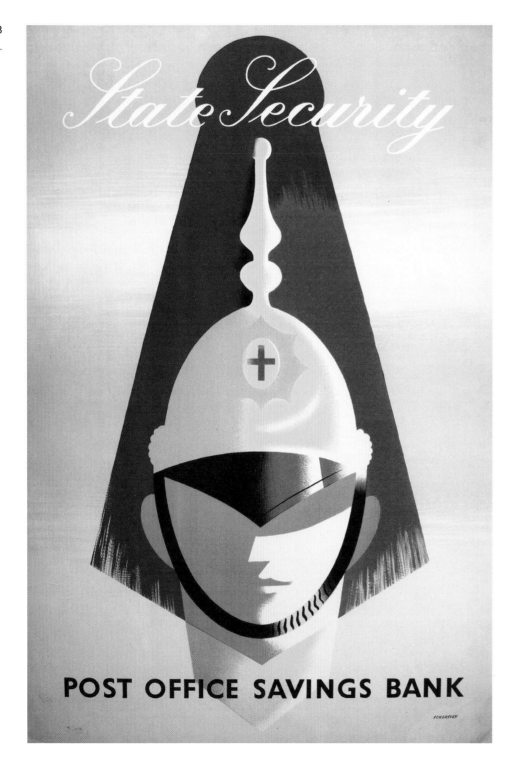

State Security
Post Office Savings Bank, 1950s
Eckersley Archive, LCC

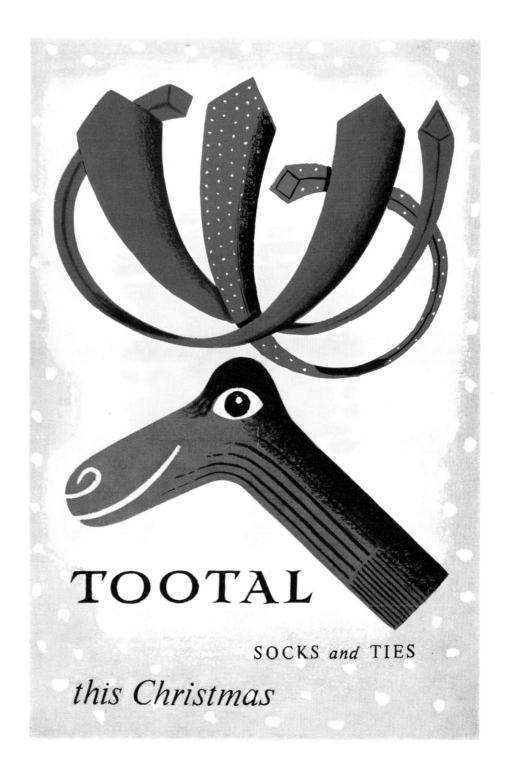

Tootal this Christmas
Point-of-sale showcard, 1950s
Eckersley Archive, LCC

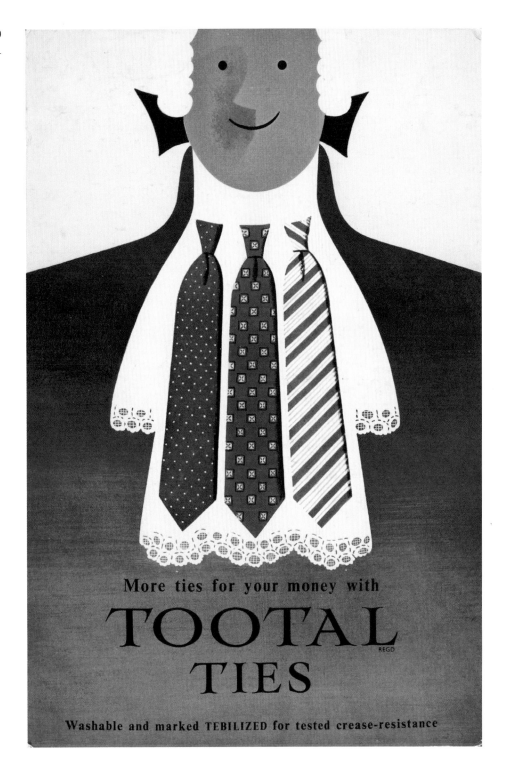

Tootal Ties
Point-of-sale showcard, 1950s
Eckersley Archive, LCC

Tootal Guaranteed Fabrics
Point-of-sale showcard, 1950s
Eckersley Archive, LCC

Lovely day for a
GUINNESS

Lovely Day for a Guinness
Guinness, 1950s
Eckersley Archive, LCC

after work
GUINNESS

ECKERSLEY

△ After Work Guinness beer mat
Guinness, 1950s
Paul and Karen Rennie collection

▷ After Work Guinness poster
Guinness, 1950s
Eckersley Archive, LCC

EVERSLEY

For Judges of Good Beer
Trumans, 1950s
Paul and Karen Rennie collection

Christmas Gifts
Simpson of Piccadilly, 1950s
Eckersley Archive, LCC

Balloon Seller
Advertising concept, c. 1950s
Eckersley Archive, LCC

from garden to tin in two hours

From Garden to Tin in Two Hours
Hartley's Peas, 1950s
Eckersley Archive, LCC

▲ **Please Pack Parcels Very Carefully**
Toby jug, GPO, 1958
Eckersley Archive, LCC

◀ **Please Pack Parcels Very Carefully**
Piggy bank, GPO, 1958
Eckersley Archive, LCC

▲ Please Pack Parcels Very Carefully
China cat, GPO, 1958
Eckersley Archive, LCC

Please pack parcels very carefully

▲ Please Pack Parcels Very Carefully
Staffordshire dog, GPO, 1958
Eckersley Archive, LCC

▶ Properly Packed Parcels Please
GPO, 1959
Eckersley Archive, LCC

▶ Post Early for Christmas
GPO, 1954
Eckersley Archive, LCC

It's time to be

buying your

Christmas gifts for posting overseas

Latest posting dates will be displayed
in this Post Office from early October

Louis Armstrong

world famous jazz trumpeter

now records exclusively for

The Decca Record Company Ltd., London, S.W.9

Christmas Overseas Posting
GPO, 1950s
Eckersley Archive, LCC

Louis Armstrong
Decca Records, black and white press advertising,
1950s
Eckersley Archive, LCC

Holiday Runabout Tickets
British Railways, 1950s
Eckersley Archive, LCC

Holiday Runabout Tickets
British Railways, 1950s
Eckersley Archive, LCC

Geneva
Pakistan International Airways, 1958
Eckersley Archive, LCC

London
Pakistan International Airways, 1958
Eckersley Archive, LCC

Tom Eckersley conceptualised a series of
posters for PIA that showed an internationally
recognisable archetype looking to the skies.
The series also included posters for Rome
and Beirut.

ECKERSLEY

NATIONS
NATIONS
NATIONS
NATIONS
NATIONS
NATIONS
NATIONS
NATIONS
NATIONS
NATIONS

EIGHTY-TWO

UNITED NATIONS DAY

TO KEEP THE PEACE

OCTOBER
24

 FOURTEEN YEARS OLD

PREPARED FOR THE FOREIGN OFFICE BY THE CENTRAL OFFICE OF INFORMATION   PRINTED FOR H. M. STATIONERY OFFICE BY FOSH & CROSS LTD., LONDON. 51-3187

United Nations Day
Foreign Office, 1959
Eckersley Archive, LCC

Railway Excursions poster
British Railways, 1950s
Eckersley Archive, LCC

Original Christmas card design
Tom and Daisy Eckersley, 1951
Paul and Karen Rennie Collection

This design also appeared on
a souvenir melamine tray, available
in association with the Festival of
Britain during 1951.

CHAPTER 6

1960s
Modern Design and Modern Life

THE 1960S was a period in which Tom Eckersley consolidated his professional standing through the combination of teaching and design. Indeed, in 1963 he was appointed Royal Designer for Industry.

The Royal Designers form an important part of the Royal Society of Arts. The organisation itself was founded in 1754 by William Shipley as the Society for the Encouragement of Arts, Manufactures and Commerce. It was granted a Royal Charter in 1847 and the right to use the term 'Royal' in its title in 1908.

In 1936, the distinction of Royal Designer was established to be awarded to a maximum of 200 individuals at any one time, on the basis of their sustained design excellence and work of aesthetic value and significant benefit to society.

Keep Britain Tidy (detail), Central Office of Information, 1963
Eckersley Archive, LCC. Full poster on page 177.

The RDI is the highest accolade for designers in the UK. Royal Designers are 'responsible for designing the world around us, enriching our cultural heritage, driving innovation, inspiring creativity in others and improving our quality of life.'

The distinction, and its association with the RSA, makes the connection between art-design and life explicit and builds upon the founding moral principles of the eighteenth-century philosophical Enlightenment.

Tom Eckersley's appointment was only the second awarded specifically for poster design; the first was to his friend Abram Games.

Teaching in the 1960s
London College of Printing at the Elephant and Castle
The opportunity to consolidate the entire school on one site became possible as part of the post-war redevelopment of south London. Originally, a site on the South Bank had been identified for the school. But the

Festival of Britain in 1951 and the development of the Shell Centre forced a reconsideration. Eventually, a site was found as part of the comprehensive redevelopment of the Elephant and Castle intersection in Southwark.

The London County Council and their architects undertook the development of the site and proposed a tower block, workshop units and communal area, along with the statutory provision for car parking! The new school was to be made available by 1963.

The details of the plan were worked out in consultation with the school, led by Ellis Thirkettle, principal. A projection of increasing student numbers and a requirement for new technical training shaped the detailed specification of the building. The allocation of space at the new site became, inevitably perhaps, something of a political battle between different interests within the school. Nowhere was this more evident than in the provision of new studio space for the School of Design under Tom Eckersley.

With his professional background and his European connections cemented through the AGI, it was not entirely surprising that Eckersley was invited during 1957 to begin planning the new Design School as part of the preparation for moving from Back Hill to the Elephant and Castle. His own education had been in the beaux-arts traditions of commercial art. However, he had acknowledged the ideas of the continental modernists and had been at the forefront of integrating these ideas into a British context, where they became part of a sophisticated visual language derived from a more collegiate and interdisciplinary approach. Elsewhere, and in different contexts, the typographer John Lewis and Ashley Havinden had also made important contributions to this effort.

The educational ideas that Eckersley was exploring were given official and formal expression in the first report of the National Advisory Council on Art Education in 1960. The report, prepared by Sir William Coldstream, gave unprecedented freedom to individual tutors and institutions to shape the new National Diploma (DipAD). Part of the Coldstream reform was to give individual institutions more autonomy in the construction and management of their courses. This was counterbalanced by the beginnings of a more robust system of peer review. The Design School at LCP was substantially strengthened by the presence of Ashley Havinden and F.H.K. Henrion as governors.

The Coldstream Report marked the beginning of a more widely available conceptual training for artists and designers in Britain. It acknowledged the lead, at post-graduate level, given by Robin Darwin at the Royal College of Art and sought to integrate the more speculative and philosophical skills of creative direction into the studio. The studio environments were lightened, at the Elephant, by an embrace of a more playful and speculative approach to problem-solving in design.

The Design School promoted graphic design as a problem-solving activity that drew on a range of skills and technologies to achieve its objectives. Eckersley imagined the studio spaces of the school as an environment where different solutions to a particular brief could be assembled. Thereafter the merits of each could be discussed and improvements made as required. The idea of the studio as laboratory was a radical departure from the beaux-arts tradition of specialisation through craft. So too was the relatively relaxed and informal teaching environment favoured by Eckersley. This produced a community, in theory at least, where problems were shared and ideas exchanged.

The new school proposed a series of workshops that would support the traditional skills of commercial printing and also develop the more agile and immediate possibilities of screen printing.

In its earliest form, silk-screen printing had developed from the tradition of cut stencils to produce repeated designs. In the 1930s and 1940s screen printing

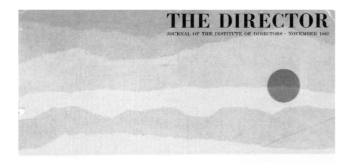

The Director magazine cover
Institute of Directors, 1962
Eckersley Archive, London College of Communication

remained a low-tech and craft-based process that involved stretching a fabric screen across a frame and cutting the stencils by hand. In practice, the frame helped keep the stencil in shape during a process of repeated printing. Also, the screen engaged gently with the paper or fabric upon which the print was being made.

The stencil evolved from the basic cut-paper stencil to cut-film and photo-stencil variations. Forcing the ink through the stencil produced a solid layer of ink onto the paper, which gave a distinctive and contemporary-looking flat-colour effect. The contemporary appeal of screen-print effects was further enhanced by the development of brighter printing inks, fluorescent colours and matt effects.

During the 1950s, a number of technical developments began to transform the process of screen printing so that it became commercially viable for short-run posters and other visual material. Not only was this useful within the increasingly dynamic retail environments of the post-war consumer boom, screen printing also became a standard for art-school production. In addition to helping students realise their projects, the process could also be used to create the many kinds of posters required around the campus and building of the greatly expanded college environments of the 1960s.

In the course of the 1960s and 1970s, screen printing became an increasingly mechanical process. The technical developments that had transformed colour lithography, during the 1940s, from a craft process into a photo-mechanical activity were applied to screen printing. In the course of the 1960s, the silk-screen print became a staple of every aspect of the burgeoning youth and countercultural scene in Britain, from T-shirts to posters.

151

The advent of screen printing into the art-school environment changed the way that Eckersley worked. He became interested in the effects of overlaying colours and using simple blocks of flat colour to create a sense of form in three dimensions. He would continue working with screen-print designs for the remainder of his career. At LCP, Eckersley produced a series of posters for display across the school that promoted a variety of good causes and best practices.

The Design School at the London College of Printing and the direction of its course under Tom Eckersley provided the first opportunity for this kind of training for undergraduates. The studio environment was enlivened through Eckersley's choices of visiting lecturers, who helped create the experimental atmosphere of a laboratory. The house style at the Elephant and Castle became quite distinct from that at either the still tweedily styled Royal College of Art, or that from the Central School of Art and Design, where Herbert Spencer and Anthony Froshaug had promoted a more formally rigorous expression of graphic design based on precise numerical specification. At Chelsea the typographer Edward Wright developed a design course with more evident links to photography and to architecture.

At the Elephant, Frederick Lambert became Eckersley's deputy and Mary Kessell, teacher and former war artist, introduced elements of life drawing and a fine-art sensibility to the studio.

In 1966, Eckersley and Mary Kessell were married. He recognised Mary as a kindred spirit, recalling that she had come from a similar sort of background to his own. She was an exact contemporary of Tom's and had attended the Central School in London. She had begun her professional career by illustrating books and

was appointed at the end of the Second World War an Official War Artist, one of only three women to be selected for this work. She was posted to Germany, where her work included recording the liberation of the Bergen-Belsen concentration camps and the devastation of various German cities. This experience had a profound impact on Mary.

After the war, Mary worked for the Shell design studio and with the Needlework Development Scheme to provide schemes that could be elaborated as part of the technical formation in art schools of this activity. She was an accomplished mural artist and produced mural paintings for the Westminster Hospital and for the ICI headquarters in Millbank, London.

At the end of the 1950s, Mary joined the teaching staff of the Central School, before joining the LCP in the early 1960s.

Later, Tom was instrumental in helping his RoSPA colleagues, Leonard Cusden and Desmond Moore, join the staff at LCP.

The tutors and students at the LCP embraced Anglo-European sophistication and mixed it with an American beat-scene influence. The result was certainly more countercultural and left-leaning than either the St Martin's Soho coffee-bar scene, or Kensington's embrace of traditional jazz and American pop culture at the Royal College.

The new site in South London also provided a context of reconstruction and social mobility that was obviously missing from the more central locations of Soho and Kensington. The location also chimed with the more acute political engagement promoted by the progressive origins of the course. Eckersley's Methodist upbringing had made him tolerant of Nonconformist and political radicalism. He always prompted students to think differently. This iconoclastic tendency was reflected in the college magazine *Typos* and in the activities of its staff. Desmond Jeffrey, Keith Cunningham and Ken Campbell, all editors, sustained their idealism beyond the college.

The early 1960s witnessed a dramatic expansion in the design environment. The consumer boom of the 1960s was launched by the beginnings of mass-circulation lifestyle magazine supplements at the *Sunday Times* (where David King, from Back Hill, helped define the visual style of the magazine as different and separate from the paper) and at *The Observer*. The magazine environment became more dynamic generally, with many more titles available. The beginnings of *Nova* and *Esquire* and the transformations at *Queen* were all powered by a new generation of designers and photographers schooled by Tom Eckersley.

The commercial endorsements of popular television began to have an impact on the high streets of Britain as the advertising industry began to reinvent itself along the lines of a sharp, street-credible intelligence that combined American dynamism with English wit. The creation of the annual showcase of the educational charity Design and Art Direction (D&AD) in 1964 acknowledged this change of status.

It's evident from the early D&AD annuals that one of the first firms to ride this wave successfully was the partnership established by Alan Fletcher, Colin Forbes and Bob Gill. Fletcher had been to the Central School and thence to the RCA and to Yale. Forbes was another Central School alumni, and Gill was from the USA. Eventually, and with the addition of Theo Crosby and Kenneth Grange, the firm became Pentagram.

By the end of the decade the social changes outlined earlier had kicked in and opportunities for a form of graphic design that served the interests of the music, fashion and other youth-culture environments had emerged. Some of these are reflected in Fred Lambert's annual selections in *Graphic Design Britain* of 1967 and 1970. For a measure of just how far the graphic design environment had changed in terms of style, content and tone, it is instructive to contrast the selections of D&AD, Fred Lambert and the earlier *Designers in Britain* sponsored by the Society of Industrial Artists. Former students David Hillman, by then at IPC, and David King, with Michael Rand at the *Sunday Times*, were both represented in the 1970 edition.

The dynamic reality of these changes is recalled by the phrase 'Swinging London'. For those who weren't there, a wide range of magazines, record sleeves, film clips and posters provide the substantive evidence from this period. This material speaks of the optimistic idealism of a new, young and exciting reality.

The 1960s explosion of graphic design in Britain was described by John Commander in his introduction to the survey *17 Graphic Designers, London* (1963). He acknowledged that one of the purposes of the book was to show how the scale and scope of graphic design was beginning, even at the beginning of the 1960s, to reach beyond the established limits of familiarity and the print economy.

By the end of the 1960s, graphic design in Britain had moved beyond the boundaries of the print economy and had begun to transform the visual languages of television and retail. Eventually, design would align itself with strategic issues of identity, production and consumption.

The scale and scope of Eckersley's influence in design is amply demonstrated by the consideration of the careers of some of his students at LCP. Tom Eckersley came into contact with many students and helped direct them towards a world of design that, in the 1960s at least, had begun to seem bigger in scope and more dynamic and lively in form than previously. It's testimony to Eckersley that his students transformed the world, and our experience of it, through design. Below are just three famous examples of this amazing outreach in relation to newspapers and magazines, advertising, and to restaurants and the food economy. But we'll begin by considering his son Richard.

Richard Eckersley (1941–2006)

Each of Tom Eckersley's sons with Daisy – Anthony, Richard and Paul – followed Tom into the world of design. Paul was a teacher at LCP, and Anthony made a career in advertising, but it was Richard who followed Tom most closely in combining his practice of design with life.

From 1962 to 1966, Richard attended LCP and studied for the art and design diploma. Richard's understanding of design as an expression of both the intrinsic and visible quality of thinking was further developed at Lund Humphries and in his career in the USA. Richard's contribution to the typographic presentation of academic texts was acknowledged by his appointment as Royal Designer for Industry in 1999.

David Hillman

From a modern standpoint, the newspaper and magazine world of post-war Britain is almost unrecognisable. For a start, there was just much less of everything, and with fewer pictures and much less colour. Notwithstanding its pioneer status, *Picture Post*, the photographic magazine of the 1940s and early 1950s, contrives to appear both low-res and busy, and without any of the glamour of, say, its US counterpart, *Life*.

The advent of new printing technologies made high-volume colour printing economically possible for the first time. Combined with the emergence of a new retail economy and against a backdrop of renewed confidence, publishers were able to expand their efforts through new titles to reach new segments of the market.

David Hillman, who attended LCP in the 1960s, has played a key role in the transformation of newspapers, magazine and book publishing in the UK. After starting at the *Sunday Times* magazine at the end of the 1960s, Hillman became art director of *Nova*, before joining Pentagram. More recently, he has transformed *The Guardian* newspaper and the format and presentation of art publisher Phaidon.

The colour supplements for *The Sunday Times* and *The Observer* were conceptualised as image-led lifestyle supplements to the weekly news digest of the weekend. The *Sunday Times* magazine, *Queen*, *Town* and *Nova* each extended the style and scope of what could be written about and illustrated.

The *Sunday Times*, launched in 1962 and with first-mover advantage, combined grit and glamour, using photography and illustration to document the social transformations associated with the counterculture, fashion and music. The direction of Michael Rand and David King made a virtue of the limitations of print technology and pushed a style of exaggerated contrasts and pop-style graphics.

David King had studied at Back Hill with Eckersley, Fior and Hollis. King later developed a neo-constructivist and supremely economical graphic language for the London listings magazine *City Limits*.

Nowadays, King is remembered as a pioneer collector of Soviet-period graphic design.

David Hillman took this experimental sensibility to *Nova* magazine, which applied a more impressionistic visual style to its fashion stories and helped establish the dream-like sensibility of the fashion story of the 1970s. *Nova* aligned political radicalism with the lifestyle choices devolving from the counterculture, and used design to give visual expression to these ideas.

The structural alignment between form and content evident in *Nova* was later applied by Hillman to *The Guardian*. The logic of organising content across both a vertical and horizontal axis of values is now applied to web formats.

In the circumstances, Hillman could claim to have transformed how we engage with information and understand it visually.

Charles Saatchi

Charles Saatchi attended the LCP at the end of the 1960s and, together with his brother Maurice, established the eponymous advertising agency in 1970. Nowadays, Saatchi is recognised as not only a pioneering advertising creative, but also as the most significant British patron of contemporary art.

As an advertising executive, Saatchi helped to develop the concept advertisement. This was a style of advertising in which, just as in contemporary art, the idea was foregrounded at the relative expense of technical finish.

In practical terms, this allowed for a much quicker response in the to and fro between advertisers and audience. The advent of fast advertising helped redefine the relationships between products, ideas and consumers in Britain. By a happy coincidence,

the economic productivity of this approach allowed for more work and more profit.

Ruth Rogers

Ruth, Lady Rogers, the second wife of the architect Richard Rogers, studied at LCP in 1968. At the end of the 1980s Ruth, along with Rose Gray, established the River Café in London. The restaurant drew on their personal experience of Italy and promoted quality, freshness and seasonality. In 1996, the restaurant published the first in what has become a long series of cookbooks. *The River Café Cookbooks* were notable not only for their recipes, but for the quality of their visual presentation and for their integration of parts, through design, into a coherent and meaningful lifestyle.

The Rogers' sophisticated and cosmopolitan existence, made explicit through the work-life balance evident in the studio and restaurant combination, was based on the Brumwell (DRU) and Artist Partners template of internationalist sophistication.

It's evident from these very brief notes that the scope of graphic design quickly extended during the 1960s into worlds beyond the traditional limits of the print economy. The combination of technology and ideas exemplified by each of the stories above, and across the scope of each of their activities, can be said to have transformed Britain.

The underlying seriousness of this design effort was later substantiated by significant contributions by former students beyond Back Hill and the Elephant. Ian McLaren went to the Ulm School of Design in 1959 and has travelled extensively since. Nearer home, Bill Stobbs helped redefine the courses at Maidstone and Ravensbourne. Ivan Dodd designed the Nuffield New Mathematics programme.

Tom Eckersley's efforts at the Elephant helped others shape a new world. Without his guiding intelligence the design environments of the 1960s and early 70s would have been very different.

Design Work in the 1960s
London Transport – Victoria line

The post-war reconstruction of London was framed within the concept of a greatly expanded city with 'new town' satellites. The shape of London was described in detail through the Abercrombie Plan and in various publications. In the immediate post-war era, individual car ownership remained the exception rather than the rule. Accordingly, the extension and acceleration of the transport infrastructure was planned.

Various deep underground 'tube' railways had been proposed from 1946 onwards. A line connecting Victoria to Walthamstow was recommended in 1948 by the working party of the British Transport Commission. A Private Bill was introduced into Parliament in 1955 and described a line from Victoria to Walthamstow (Wood Street).

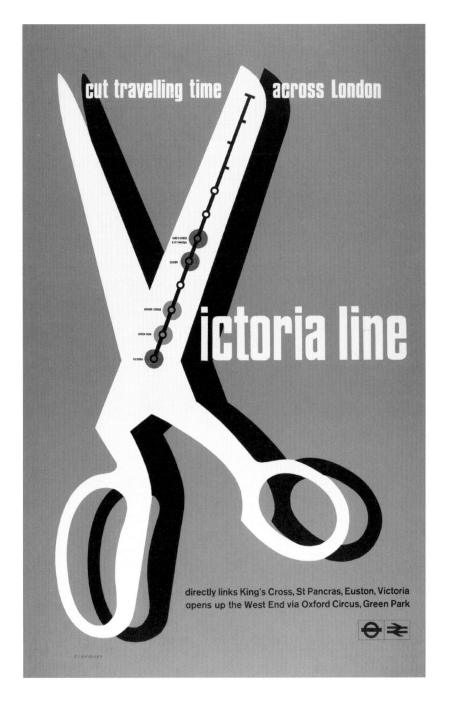

▲ Victoria Line
London Transport, 1969
Eckersley Archive, LCC

▷ Tile design,
Finsbury Park station,
1968

Construction was begun in 1962 on the initial Walthamstow to Victoria section, opening from Walthamstow to Highbury on 1 September 1968. In August 1967 the government gave approval for the Brixton extension. In June 1968 a proposal to build a station at Pimlico was approved. The entire Walthamstow–Brixton line was completed in 1972.

The stations of the Victoria line were designed, where possible, as interchange stations. The idea was to have fewer stations with larger capacities that could feed passengers onto other lines. As the city grew larger, the underground had to accelerate, accommodate more passengers and integrate better with the existing lines.

I have already mentioned Frank Pick, of London Transport, in relation to design integration and standardisation across the London transport system.

It seems obvious that, deep underground and without the usual markers of specific location, passengers might easily become confused as to where exactly they are in relation to the surface detail of the city.

The early stations of the underground railway used colour and decoration as place-markers for each station. Tile decoration was chosen as providing an economical and efficient finish that was hard-wearing, reflective and hygienic. Frank Pick had managed to combine integration and standardisation with an element of local identity, expressed through poster displays.

The 1960s Victoria line revisited this idea by creating a specific tiled identity for each station against a background of more rigorously standardised typography and engineering finish. The overall design of the station interior was overseen by Misha Black of the DRU and used an architectural palette of industrial greys. Against this backdrop of relatively austere and consistent station environments, the tile identities allowed for a short burst of colour and wit.

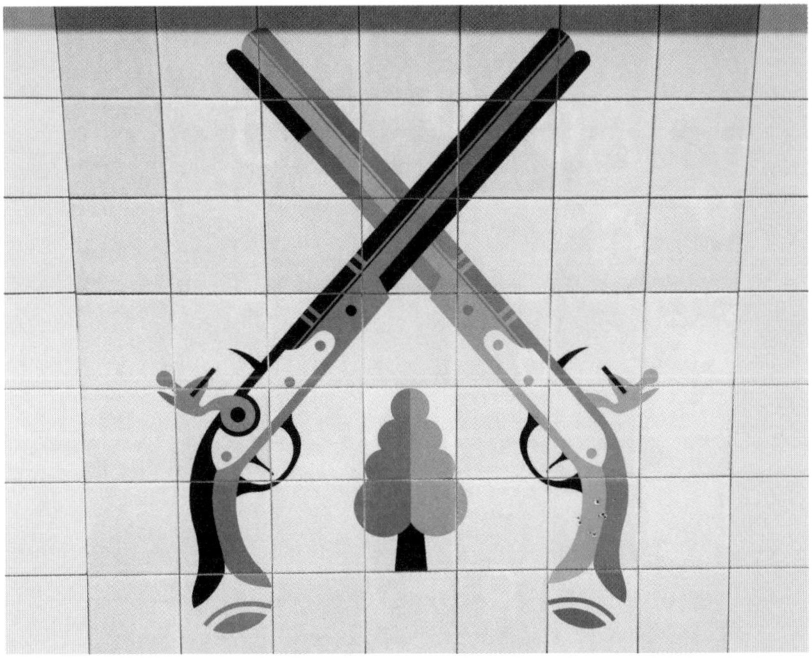

Tom Eckersley was among the designers chosen to elaborate the tile identities for the Victoria line. The stations of the original line and their artist designers are, travelling southbound from Walthamstow:

Walthamstow – Julia Black and
   William Morris
Blackhorse Road – Hans Unger
Tottenham Hale – Edward Bawden
Seven Sisters – Hans Unger
Finsbury Park – Tom Eckersley

▲▲ Tile design, King's Cross St Pancras station, 1968

▲ Tile design, Euston station, 1968

Highbury and Islington – Edward Bawden
King's Cross St Pancras – Tom Eckersley
Euston – Tom Eckersley
Warren Street – Crosby Fletcher Forbes
   (Pentagram)
Oxford Circus – Hans Unger
Green Park – Hans Unger
Victoria – Edward Bawden
Vauxhall – George Smith
Stockwell – Abram Games
Brixton – Hans Unger

1960s Poster Design

Against the backdrop of increasing teaching responsibilities at LCP, Eckersley's poster design work was necessarily reduced. Nevertheless, throughout the 1960s he continued to work with London Transport and for the General Post Office. His designs reflect his interest in the technical possibilities of screen printing and in the overlaying effects made possible by the new processes of graphic reproduction. He also undertook work for the Design Council and for the United Nations.

Eckersley acknowledged that his association with LCP afforded him the luxury of being able to design his own style without the compromises that are part and parcel of work in the commercial sector. This allowed him to follow his distinctive approach to its logical conclusion.

Several of his posters are notable for their persistent flattening out of the images, so they become uncompromisingly two-dimensional, and for their play on depth, produced by a tonal difference created by overprinting colours. This is especially striking in Lincolnshire for British Railways (1961), where the volumes of the trees and buildings are set within a determinedly flat plane. A similar effect of space is evident in the cover design for *Director*, where the torn-paper shapes of the trees and sky contrast with precision cut-outs of the viaduct and train. The majority of Eckersley's posters after 1960 achieve their effect by denying, ever more rigidly, the volumes and spaces of binocular vision.

Eckersley's posters created their own world: a world described by flat colours, precise outlines and simplified shapes that we have learned to decode. Nowhere is this more evident than in the 'Hollywood Greats' series of portraits. The most successful of these – Harold Lloyd, Groucho and Garbo – show the star by the angle of the head, the shape of the spectacles, an allusion to the shape and weight of the unseen body. None of these images would make sense to someone who had no prior knowledge of the subject matter – an assumption that allowed Eckersley to take risks, and to reduce images to their essentials.

TOM ECKERSLEY

till Grafiska Institutets Stjärnseminarium
30, 31 maj, 1 juni 1960

Den berömde engelske reklamkonstnären leder årets seminarium
för nordiska grafiska formgivare

Kursavgift kronor 225:––, inkluderande kursmiddag

Anmälan före den 1 maj Stockholm 60 02 13

Tom Eckersley exhibition poster
Grafiska Institute, Stockholm, 1960
Eckersley Archive, LCC

The Art of Persuasion

A publicity design exhibition by members of the Society of Industrial Artists

May 25 - June 15   Mon - Fri 9.30-7   Sat 9.30-12.30

De La Rue House 84-6 Regent Street W1   Admission free

The Art of Persuasion exhibition poster
Society of Industrial Artists, 1960
Eckersley Archive, LCC

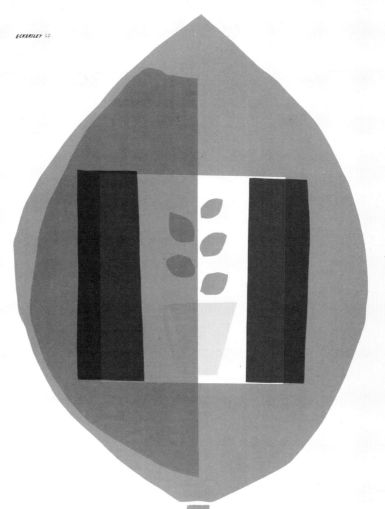

ECKERSLEY 62.

WEEKEND LIVING

furnishing ideas for a country cottage

THE DESIGN CENTRE
Haymarket London SW1

27 February to 8 April

9.30 am to 5.30 pm Monday to Saturday
Until 9.0 pm Wednesday and Thursday

Weekend Living exhibition poster
The Design Centre, 1960s
Eckersley Archive, LCC

Printed invitation
London College of Printing, 1967
Eckersley Archive, LCC

Printed invitation
London College of Printing, 1960s
Eckersley Archive, LCC

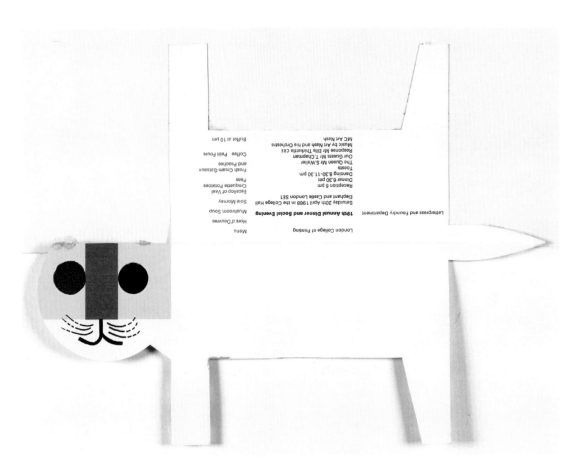

◀ Printed invitation
London College of Printing, 1969
Eckersley Archive, LCC

▶ Printed invitation
London College of Printing, 1969
Eckersley Archive, LCC

Second Annual Dinner and Social Evening

London College of Printing
Machine Printing and Foundry Department

The Surrey Tavern, The Oval, Kennington, London SE11
Saturday 18th April 1970

Reception 6 pm
Dinner 6.30 pm
Dancing 8.30 pm to midnight

Toasts
The Queen   Mr Stan Waller
The Guests   Mr Tom Chapman
Response   Mr Leslie Owens
               Mr Arnold Quick

Music during dinner and for dancing
will be provided by Art Nash

Master of Ceremonies Bert Steward

Menu

Minestrone Soup

Fillet of Sole Veronique

Saddle of Lamb
Green Garden Peas
Braised Carrots
Roast and Parsley Potatoes

Mandarin Oranges
Ice Cream

Coffee

Printed invitation
London College of Printing, 1970
Eckersley Archive, LCC

Printed invitation
London College of Printing, 1970s
Eckersley Archive, LCC

Investment Account
Post Office Savings Bank, 1960s
Eckersley Archive, LCC

National Savings Bank
at the Post Office

Investment Account

NOW UP TO 7½%

Interest
Post Office Savings Bank, 1960s
Eckersley Archive, LCC

mind
that
door

opening carriage doors before the train stops

CAUSES ACCIDENTS

please stand away from platform edge

BRITISH RAILWAYS

Mind That Door
British Railways, 1960
Eckersley Archive, LCC

See London's country

by Green Rover ticket

Unlimited travel for a day over 1400 miles of green Country Bus routes **5/-**
children 2/6

Please write for a free map and leaflet to the Publicity Officer, London Transport, Griffith House, 280 Marylebone Road, N.W.1.

Green Rover Ticket
London Transport, 1959
London Transport Museum

THE LONDON MUSEUM is the Londoner's own museum – the everyday London scene, both indoor and out, from pre-history onwards, displayed in London's friendliest royal residence, Kensington Palace. You can also see the superb State Apartments, with their William Kent decorations, and the charming Orangery which Wren built for Queen Anne. Open free Monday to Saturday 10-6, Sunday 2-6.

Underground to Queensway or High Street Kensington. Any bus along Kensington High Street, Kensington Road or Kensington Church Street

The London Museum
London Transport, 1963
Eckersley Archive, LCC

In 1871 CUTTY SARK, heavily laden with the first tea crop, raced from Shanghai in 108 days. She carried 32,000 square feet of sail and was capable of $17\frac{1}{2}$ knots. She now rests dry berthed at Greenwich, the last of the clippers, sole survivor of an age.

The free leaflet *A Day Out at Greenwich* describes the many interesting things to be explored there. Please write for a copy to the Public Relations Officer, 55 Broadway, Westminster, S.W.1, or ask at any London Transport Enquiry Office.

Cutty Sark
London Transport, 1965
Eckersley Archive, LCC

WN65T   7] x 4]   Catalogues 1964   P39m2

Eckersley

for best results

WINSOR & NEWTON
ARTISTS' MATERIALS

Winsor & Newton Ltd Wealdstone Harrow Middlesex

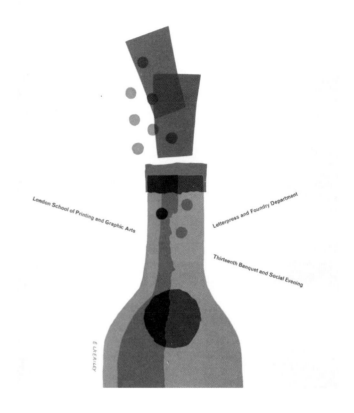

London School of Printing and Graphic Arts

Letterpress and Foundry Department

Thirteenth Banquet and Social Evening

E ECKERSLEY

For Best Results
Winsor & Newton, black and white
newspaper advertising, 1960s
Eckersley Archive, LCC

Social evening poster
London College of Printing, 1960s
Eckersley Archive, LCC

Eastern and North-Eastern England **1961**

holiday haunts

BRITISH RAILWAYS   PRICE 2/-

ECKERSLEY

holiday haunts 1961 EASTERN & NORTH-EASTERN ENGLAND **no. 3**

Holiday Haunts
British Railways pamphlet, 1965
Eckersley Archive, LCC

ROUND LONDON SIGHTSEEING TOUR
Two hours, twenty miles of the City and the West End
from Buckingham Palace Road (near Victoria Station)
every day, hourly from 10 00 to 16 00 except 13 00
Fares: adults 6/- children 3/- Seats are not bookable

See London by Bus
London Transport, 1969
Eckersley Archive, LCC

Keep Britain Tidy
Central Office of Information, 1963
Eckersley Archive, LCC

Brochure cover design
Motor Trade Executive,
1964
Eckersley Archive, LCC

mte

MOTOR TRADE EXECUTIVE · AUGUST 1966   JOURNAL OF THE MAA

Brochure cover design
Motor Trade Executive,
1966
Eckersley Archive, LCC

mte 37

MOTOR TRADE EXECUTIVE   JANUARY 1963

Brochure cover design
Motor Trade Executive,
1963
Eckersley Archive, LCC

mte *49*

MOTOR TRADE EXECUTIVE · JANUARY 1964

ECKERSLEY

**Brochure cover design
Motor Trade Executive,
1964**
Eckersley Archive, LCC

CHAPTER 7

1970s and beyond
Retirement and Reputation

THE 1970S were the decade when the idealism that had distinguished the post-war settlement began to turn. Eckersley's career at LCP continued, but against a background of increasing administrative upheaval.

Inevitably, most of this was derived from the requirement to teach more students with fewer resources. But Eckersley was also unhappy about the increasing academicisation of the art school. Recalling his own experience in Lancashire, he was conscious of his very good fortune in having been able to pursue his interest in poster design at Salford in spite of a childhood of illness and missed school.

He believed that graphic design was, at its heart, a relatively simple and straightforward activity. That didn't mean that it was easy, nor that it didn't require careful consideration. But mostly it involved listening to the client and giving consideration to the parts within the context of the whole.

Eckersley's own design work, in posters, entered its final and mature phase. He produced a number of posters for the college as well as for London Transport, the World Wildlife Fund and later for the National Business Calendar Awards. Between them, these patrons would sustain his professional activities until 1997, the year of his death.

He was supported in his work by the team of technical colleagues at LCP. Philip Rayner, Graham Pullen, Errol White, Gordon Baxter and Anthony Braithwaite each helped Tom achieve what he wanted from screen printing. David Sinfield advised him on the specialised aspects of typographic design in his posters. Frank Dyson, Arthur Lloyd and Jim McBride, colleagues from graphic reproduction, also helped as the editions scaled up.

Tom Eckersley exhibition poster (detail), Yale Centre for British Art, 1981
Eckersley Archive, LCC. Full poster on page 204.

Eckersley and his colleagues produced a coherent body of work for the college and were able to project that identity beyond the immediate vicinity of the Elephant and Castle. He also conceptualised a series of decorative prints based on the distinctive characteristics of Hollywood film stars, discussed at the end of the previous chapter. These were made available to wine bars and other locations that required inexpensive decoration.

London Transport Collection, London Transport, 1975
Eckersley Archive, LCC

Tom Eckersley retired from LCP in 1976. Mary Kessell, his second wife, died in 1977.

Work for London Transport, 1970s and Beyond

From 1975–1977 the Piccadilly line was extended westwards to serve London Heathrow airport and each of its passenger terminals.

As part of the visual identity for the international terminal, Tom Eckersley designed a mural based on the tail fins of the Anglo-French supersonic aeroplane Concorde. He produced a limited-edition screen print of the mural as a commemorative gift to guests at the opening of the station. His mural design for Heathrow was influenced by the famous Concorde stamps designed by David Gentleman, scaled up to super-graphics size as conceptualised by Edward Wright.

Edward Wright was another outsider modernist from the north-west, this time from Liverpool and with Latin American ancestry. Wright was invited by Anthony Froshaug to teach typography at the Central School in London. He was linked to the Back Hill period of Tom Eckersley's career at LCP through the association of Richard Hollis and other colleagues. Indeed, Edward Wright was given a poster credit in Eckersley's 1954 book *Poster Design*.

Wright was a significant member of the Independent Group of artists and theorists who launched a pop sensibility into British culture at the beginning of the 1960s. His great contribution was to imagine typography as an expression of a sensitive but excitingly scaled element of the urban spectacular in

Britain. His proposals for brightly coloured typography provided a different kind of enhancement and place-making from that proposed by architectural modernists working in the Brutalist style of the 1960s.

Eckersley produced poster designs at regular intervals for London Transport until 1995, two years before his death.

In addition to this work for London Transport, posters for the annual exhibition of National Business Calendar Awards provided Eckersley with the opportunity to design posters and logos for the awards committee, with the direction of Julian Royle, for over twenty years.

In 1994, Julian said that he was always impressed by Eckersley's direct approach, economy of concept and his ability to get to the heart of the message. Every piece of work went straight to the point, while also suggesting intriguing lateral associations.

Valedictories

In 1975, a year before his retirement from lecturing, Tom was the subject of a retrospective and valedictory exhibition at LCP. This provided the basis for the public-facing exhibition of his and Mary Kessell's work at Camden Arts Centre in 1980. Thereafter, his posters were routinely exhibited around the country in a series of more or less annual exhibitions. This provided the background context for the valedictory period of his career.

The Camden exhibition subsequently travelled to Norwich, Yale University in the USA, Edinburgh and back to Salford, bringing Eckersley's career full circle in a sense.

He also had exhibitions at Newcastle Polytechnic in 1983, Maidstone College of Art in 1985 and at Oxford Polytechnic and Duncan of Jordanstone College of Art, Dundee, during 1986. He enjoyed designing the posters for these exhibitions.

Tom Eckersley: Past and Present exhibition poster
Duncan of Jordanstone College of Art and Design, Dundee, 1986
Eckersley Archive, LCC

Eckersley recognised the value of exhibitions and the show-and-tell of art schools from his own experiences at Salford and at Back Hill and the Elephant. He was happy for his work to be exhibited at different art schools around the country, sometimes in association with various international colleagues. He was also happy to attend, and to speak of his career and methods to the next generation of students.

The London College of Printing again held an exhibition of Tom's work in 1992; this was formalised with the publication of a hardback catalogue titled *His Graphic Work* by the London Institute in 1994. A further recognition was bestowed when the gallery space at the LCP was formally named after Tom Eckersley in 1994. The gallery was made substantially larger during the redevelopment of the college buildings at the end of the twentieth century.

Design Legacies

Writing in 1994, Alan Fletcher, founding partner of Fletcher Forbes Gill and later Pentagram, recalled that while studying at the Central School, his design education had been formed in part by looking at posters, mostly by Tom Eckersley, on London Underground's Central Line.

Fletcher was immediately struck by Eckersley's ability to combine two disparate ideas into a coherent, distinct and meaningful synthesis. It was, said Fletcher, a kind of magic.

Fletcher instantly abandoned his John Minton period, which had been preceded for a while by his Edward Bawden period, and began his Tom Eckersley period. Years later, he wrote that he was probably 'still in it'.

Eckersley was a thoughtful and considered designer; an intelligent if not an intellectual designer. He always considered the context of where his work would be displayed, and the prospective audience as described by his client and brief, in the elaboration of his designs. He was entirely pragmatic in his design choices and was slightly suspicious of the increasingly academic

approach to design education. He understood, from his own experience, the need to be open to serendipity and chance … especially in relation to the unexpected visual effects deriving from technical changes and mishaps, as evidenced in some of his RoSPA posters. No doubt he never forgot the opportunity afforded him, through design, to move beyond his family's difficult and uncertain economic circumstances.

Eckersley's career began when poster design was understood as a kind of bridge between art and commerce, but the community of practice supported through this patronage remained relatively small. In the 1930s, Tom worked with his design partner Eric Lombers and for a handful of patrons.

The advent of the Second World War provided for a rapid expansion of design activities in support of every aspect of the war effort and then in relation to post-war reconstruction. The design community was significantly enhanced by the integration of émigré designers into its ranks along with members of a new generation. The wartime design community re-formed itself internationally, through its links with the AGI and in relation to increasing commercial activity in Britain, through the formation of multi-disciplinary agencies such as the DRU and Artist Partners.

By the 1960s, the kind of independent and autonomous design activity imagined by Eckersley in the 1930s had become possible. His position at LCP allowed him a special role in the promotion of an expanded practice in graphic design. Eventually, Eckersley and his students would transform almost every aspect of British life through the application of design to a range of activities extending beyond advertising and propaganda. In this context, he helped to reposition design as a meta-level activity of organisation that increasingly shaped the experience of everyday life.

The professional significance of Tom Eckersley's contribution to poster design was recognised through the various awards conferred upon him. Furthermore, the personal esteem in which he was regarded was evidenced through the valedictory exhibitions that celebrated his life and work. No one could claim that Tom Eckersley wasn't recognised or that he had fallen into obscurity in his lifetime ... the exact opposite is true. The advent of the visual user interface and the digital realm has given his work and approach a new significance.

He remained throughout a modest and very private individual who retained the affection of colleagues throughout his career.

This book, I hope, provides a suitable and appropriately positive account of Tom Eckersley's great contribution to British life and design.

TOM ECKERSLEY

Posters and other graphic work

Exhibition catalogue
Camden Arts Centre, 1980
Eckersley Archive, LCC

Social evening poster
London College of Printing, 1970s
Eckersley Archive, LCC

Social evening poster
London College of Printing, 1970s
Eckersley Archive, LCC

London College of Printing

**ANNUAL
DINNER
AND
SOCIAL
EVENING**

The Penthouse Suite
John Barker & Co Ltd Kensington
Saturday 27 March. 6.30 pm
Tickets from Ron Miller
Machine Printing and Foundry

Designed by Tom Eckersley and printed at the London College of Printing

**Social evening poster
London College of Printing, 1970s**
Eckersley Archive, LCC

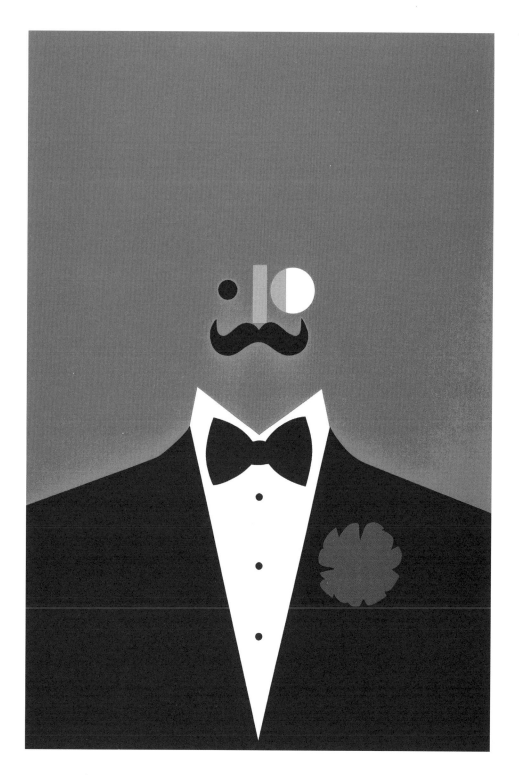

Social evening poster, collage maquette
London College of Printing, 1970s
Eckersley Archive, LCC

Long hair is dangerous

Should the class lecturer consider
a hair style is dangerous, the student
must take precautions stipulated by him.
Students refusing to do so must not
operate a machine or process

Designed by Tom Eckersley and printed at the London College of Printing

Long Hair is Dangerous
London College of Printing poster, 1970
Eckersley Archive, LCC

urgent

please
return
that
overdue
library
book
now

Urgent: Please Return That
Overdue Library Book Now
London College of Printing poster, 1970
Eckersley Archive, LCC

ECKERSLEY

keep an eye
on valuables
don't leave
them around...

Keep an Eye on Valuables
London College of Printing, 1970s
Eckersley Archive, LCC

College Printing Historical Society

J H MASON
Scholar-Printer 1875-1951

a lecture to be given by Leslie Owens
College Lecture Theatre
London College of Printing
Elephant and Castle
6 pm Wednesday 30 March 1977

Designed by Tom Eckersley and printed at the London College of Printing

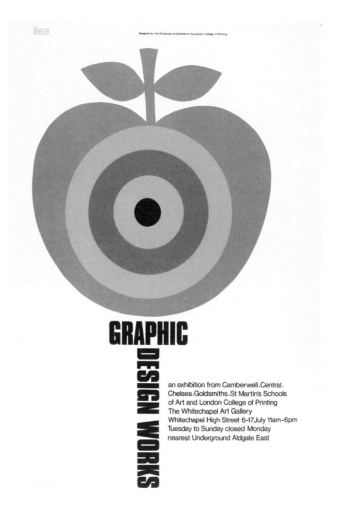

ilea

Designed by Tom Eckersley and printed at the London College of Printing

GRAPHIC DESIGN WORKS

an exhibition from Camberwell, Central,
Chelsea, Goldsmiths, St Martin's Schools
of Art and London College of Printing
The Whitechapel Art Gallery
Whitechapel High Street 6–17 July 11am–6pm
Tuesday to Sunday closed Monday
nearest Underground Aldgate East

J.H. Mason lecture poster
London College of Printing, 1977
Eckersley Archive, LCC

Graphic Design Works exhibition poster
Inner London Education Authority, 1970s
Eckersley Archive, LCC

Extension of the Piccadilly Line to Heathrow Airport
now under construction

Heathrow Central   Hatton Cross   Hounslow West

Piccadilly Line to Heathrow
London Transport, 1970s
Eckersley Archive, LCC

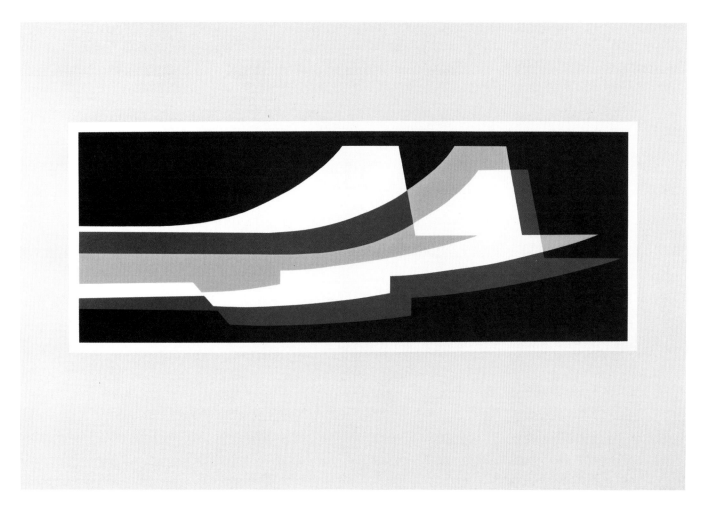

Concorde mural print
London Transport, 1970s
Eckersley Archive, LCC

Hollywood Legends screen prints
1970s
Eckersley Archive, LCC

Groucho Marx screen-print portrait
1970s
Eckersley Archive, LCC

Buster Keaton screen-print portrait
1970s
Eckersley Archive, LCC

THE KING'S TROOP

The King's Troop screen print
1977
Eckersley Archive, LCC

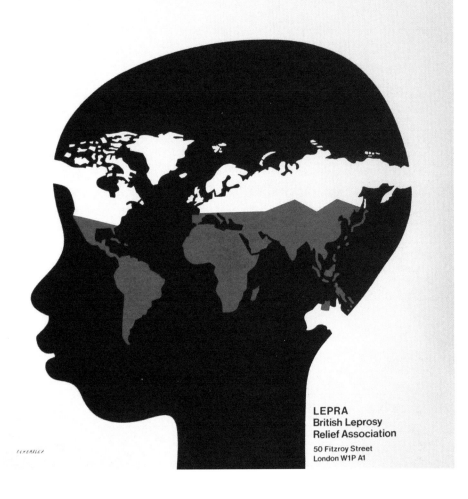

help Lepra fight Leprosy

20 MILLION PEOPLE SUFFER TODAY

LEPRA
British Leprosy
Relief Association

50 Fitzroy Street
London W1P A1

Help Lepra Fight Leprosy
LEPRA, 1975
Eckersley Archive, LCC

The Museum of London
London Transport, 1977
Eckersley Archive, LCC

TOM ECKERSLEY
Posters and other graphic work
Yale Center for British Art
December 10 1980-January 11 1981

Tom Eckersley exhibition poster
Yale Center for British Art, 1981
Eckersley Archive, LCC

Tom Eckersley Graphic Work 1934-83

25th January to 18th February 1983

Squires Building Foyer School of Graphic Design Newcastle upon Tyne Polytechnic

Tom Eckersley: Graphic Work 1934–83
exhibition poster
Newcastle Polytechnic, 1983
Eckersley Archive, LCC

Tom Eckersley: Fifty Years of Poster Design
for London Transport exhibition poster
London Transport Museum, 1984
Eckersley Archive, LCC

POSTERS TOM ECKERSLEY
13–28 February 1986 Design Department Oxford Polytechnic

Posters: Tom Eckersley exhibition poster
Oxford Polytechnic, 1986
Eckersley Archive, LCC

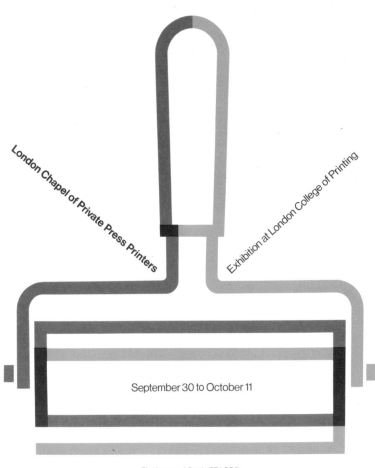

London Chapel of Private Press Printers

Exhibition at London College of Printing

September 30 to October 11

Elephant and Castle SE1 6SB

Designed by Tom Eckersley and Printed at the London College of Printing

London Chapel of Private Press Printers
exhibition poster
London College of Printing, 1986
Eckersley Archive, LCC

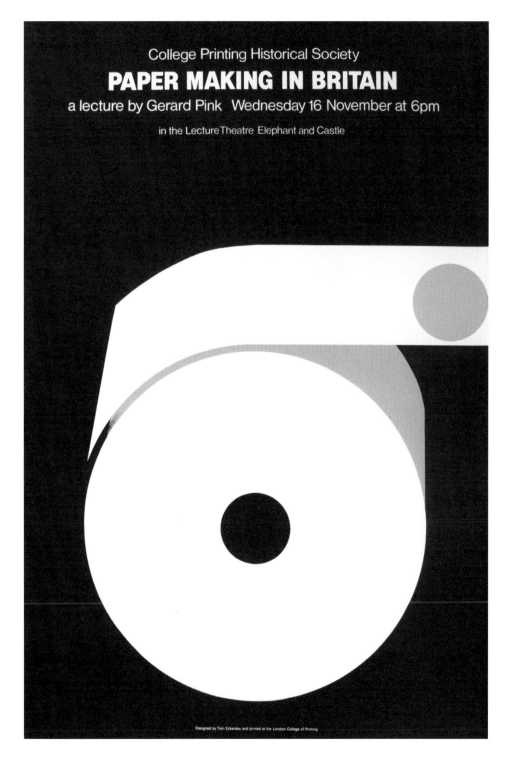

Paper Making in Britain lecture poster
London College of Printing, 1986
Eckersley Archive, LCC

Faces in the Arts   An Exhibition of photographs by Tom Evans

Camden Arts Centre Arkwright Road London NW3   April 20 to May 18 1986
Weekdays 10 30 to 5 30 Late night Wednesday until 8pm Sunday 2 to 6pm

Oganised by Hampstead Artists Council with support of London Borough of Camden and the Arkwright Arts Trust
Presented with the assistance of Polaroid UK Ltd

Arts Council
OF GREAT BRITAIN

André Kertész

An exhibition of photographs
from the Centre Georges Pompidou Paris
Serpentine Gallery Kensington Gardens W2
29 December-10 February 1980 Daily 10 00-4 30

Faces in the Arts exhibition poster
Camden Arts Centre, 1986
Eckersley Archive, LCC

André Kertész exhibition poster
Serpentine Gallery/Arts Council, 1986
Eckersley Archive, LCC

Equus
Poster for exhibition of student design
work based on the play, National
Theatre entrance foyer, 1981
Eckersley Archive, LCC

FRIENDS

FHK HENRION

TOM ECKERSLEY

50 Jahre Graphik
aus London von
TOM ECKERSLEY & FHK HENRION
5.3. bis 11.4.1993
Deutsches Plakat Museum, Essen
Rathenaustrasse 2, Theaterpassage

ECKERSLEY 91

Friends: Tom Eckersley and
F.H.K. Henrion exhibition poster
Deutsches Plakat Museum, Essen,
Germany, 1993
Eckersley Archive, LCC

Tom Eckersley: His Graphic Work
exhibition poster
London Institute, 1994
Eckersley Archive, LCC

IMPERIAL WAR MUSEUM

Weekdays 10–5 50 Sundays 2–5 50 Lambeth Road London SE1 6HZ

Underground Lambeth North or Elephant and Castle

Imperial War Museum poster
Imperial War Museum, 1981
Eckersley Archive, LCC

Man needs rain forests too
The tropical rain forests are home to half of all the
plant animal and insect species on earth, and are
watersheds that prevent erosion drought and flooding.
Help WWF save them from destruction.

WWF WORLD WILDLIFE FUND Panda House 11–13 Ockford Road Godalming Surrey

Man Needs Rain Forests Too
World Wildlife Fund, 1982
Eckersley Archive, LCC

53 83 exhibition poster
Inner London Education Authority, 1983
Eckersley Archive, LCC

Greetings
1983
Eckersley Archive, LCC

ECKERSLEY

Puffin screen print
Birds of the World series, 1986
Eckersley Archive, LCC

Selling the Sea exhibition poster
Mostyn Art Gallery, Llandudno,
1987
Eckersley Archive, LCC

Yanomamo performance poster
World Wildlife Fund, 1983
Eckersley Archive, LCC

The World Wide Fund For Nature presents

OCEAN WORLD

A musical entertainment by Peter Rose and Anne Conlon
with the choir and musicians of St Augustine's R.C.
High School Lancashire Directed by Peter Rose
Royal Festival Hall London SE1 8XX
21 September 1990 7.30pm
Tickets £5 Festival Hall Box Office Tel 071 928 8800

King George's Hall North Gate Blackburn
September 30 and October 1 7.30pm
Tickets tel 0254 582582

ECKERSLEY.

Ocean World performance poster
World Wildlife Fund, 1990
Eckersley Archive, LCC

THE
SOUTH
BANK
CENTRE

Sponsored jointly by the British Printing Industries Federation and London College of Printing

National Business Calendar Awards 1976

Exhibitions

Reed House 82 Piccadilly London W1 5–26 February

London College of Printing Back Hill EC1 2–25 March

Manchester Polytechnic Faculty of Art and Design
All Saints Manchester 1–5 March

Fielden Park College West Didsbury 15–19 March

Sponsored by the British Printing Industries Federation and the London College of Printing

National Business Calendar Awards 1977

Exhibitions

Reed House 82 Piccadilly London W1 24 February to 24 March

London College of Printing Back Hill EC1 28 March to 1 April

Manchester Polytechnic Faculty of Art and Design
All Saints Manchester 25 April to 6 May

**National Business Calendar Awards
exhibition poster, 1976**
Eckersley Archive, LCC

The National Business Calendar
Awards were set up by Julian Royle of
Royle Publishing, a long-established
and distinguished publisher of
greetings cards and other promotional
material. The calendar awards were
set up to promote the publication of
calendars as a year-long form of office
and studio advertising.

**National Business Calendar Awards
exhibition poster, 1977**
Eckersley Archive, LCC

Sponsored by the British Printing Industries Federation and the London College of Printing

National Business Calendar Awards 78

Exhibitions Kodak Photographic Gallery 246 High Holborn WC1 February 22 to March 16
London College of Printing Back Hill EC1 April 12 to April 21 And at five provincial centres

National Business Calendar Awards

Exhibitions Kodak Photographic Gallery 246 High Holborn WC1 February 21 to March 22
London College of Printing Back Hill EC1 27 March to 5 April and at certain provincial centres

Sponsored by the British Printing Industries Federation and the London College of Printing

223

National Business Calendar Awards
exhibition poster, 1978
Eckersley Archive, LCC

National Business Calendar Awards
exhibition poster, 1979
Eckersley Archive, LCC

National Business Calendar Awards 1980
at Kodak Photographic Gallery 246 High Holborn WC1 31 Jan to 18 Feb & 22 Feb to 6 Mar
London College of Printing Back Hill EC1 17 to 28 Mar and at provincial centres
Sponsored by the British Printing Industries Federation and the London College of Printing

National Business Calendar Awards 1981
Kodak Photographic Gallery 246 High Holborn WC1 29 Jan to 23 Feb and 27 Feb to 5 Mar
London College of Printing Elephant & Castle 9 Mar to 10 Apr and at provincial centres
Sponsored by the British Printing Industries Federation and the London College of Printing

National Business Calendar Awards
exhibition poster, 1980
Eckersley Archive, LCC

National Business Calendar Awards
exhibition poster, 1981
Eckersley Archive, LCC

National Business Calendar Awards
exhibition poster, 1982
Eckersley Archive, LCC

National Business Calendar Awards
exhibition poster, 1983
Eckersley Archive, LCC

National Business Calendar Awards
exhibition poster, 1985
Eckersley Archive, LCC

National Business Calendar Awards 84
Sponsored by the British Printing Industries Federation, Kodak Limited and the London College of Printing
Kodak Photographic Gallery 190 High Holborn London WC1
25 January to 1 March 1984 and at certain provincial centres

National Business Calendar Awards
exhibition poster, 1984
Eckersley Archive, LCC

Sponsored by the British Printing Industries Federation, Kodak Limited and the London College of Printing

National Business Calendar Awards 86

at the National Theatre, South Bank, London SE1

30 January to 1 March 1986 and at certain provincial centres

Sponsored by the British Printing Industries Federation, Kodak Limited and the London College of Printing

National Business Calendar Awards

Designed by Tom Eckersley and printed at the London College of Printing

Designed by Tom Eckersley and printed at the London College of Printing

National Business Calendar Awards
exhibition poster, 1986
Eckersley Archive, LCC

National Business Calendar Awards
exhibition poster, 1987
Eckersley Archive, LCC

Sponsored by the British Printing Industries Federation, Kodak Limited and the London College of Printing

National Business Calendar Awards

Business Design Centre, Upper Street, Islington Green, London N1 0QH

9th to 22nd December 1987 Weekdays 9.30am to 5.30pm

Sponsored by the British Printing Industries Federation, Kodak Limited and the London College of Printing

National Business Calendar Awards 1989

Business Design Centre, Upper Street, Islington Green, London N1 0QH

8 to 22 December 1988 weekdays 9.30am to 5.30pm

Designed by Tom Eckersley and printed in the London College of Printing

ANNIVERSARY 1968-1989

Designed by Tom Eckersley and printed at the London College of Printing

National Business Calendar Awards
exhibition poster, 1988
Eckersley Archive, LCC

National Business Calendar Awards
exhibition poster, 1989
Eckersley Archive, LCC

National Business Calendar Awards
exhibition poster, 1990
Eckersley Archive, LCC

National Business Calendar Awards
exhibition poster, 1991
Eckersley Archive, LCC

National Business Calendar Awards 92

Business Design Centre Upper Street Islington Green London N1 0QH
5 and 6 December 1991 from 9.30am to 5.30pm

Sponsored by the British Printing Industries Federation, Kodak Limited, London College of Printing and Distributive Trades.
Robert Horne, British Advertising Calendar Association and Royal Mail Stamps

National Business Calendar Awards 93

Business Design Centre Upper Street Islington Green London N1 0QH
10 and 11 December 1992 from 9.30am to 5.30pm

National Business Calendar Awards
exhibition poster, 1992
Eckersley Archive, LCC

National Business Calendar Awards
exhibition poster, 1993
Eckersley Archive, LCC

Appendix

Visual Communication, Economy, Social Progress and Intelligence

THE BACKDROP of rapid technological change has informed the widespread perception that 'first we make our tools, then our tools form us'. Nowhere is this more evident than in relation to graphic design, print culture and its link to social progress and individual development.

The association between the printing press and social progress is well-documented through histories of the scientific revolution and the eighteenth-century philosophical Enlightenment. In Britain, during the Second World War and in the 1940s there was a publishing boom associated with the elaboration of social and technical values shaping post-war reconstruction. Against this backdrop, it wasn't surprising that historians and scholars began to look again at the pamphleteering traditions of the seventeenth-century English Revolution. In the 1960s, there was another kind of publishing boom deriving from a different kind of revolution and expressed through the pop culture of alternative lifestyles.

Tom Eckersley's career in poster design spanned both of these moments and practically all of the major technical developments in modern printing. When he began designing posters, during the 1930s, he worked against a backdrop of colour lithography understood as a slightly mysterious craft process. Later, in the 1940s, some of the craft was superseded by technical specification in photo-mechanical and offset lithography. In the 1950s and 1960s, silk-screen printing brought designers and technicians together in the print studio. In the 1980s, Eckersley was able to witness the widespread advance of digital processes into the world of design.

Writing in 1954, Eckersley drew attention to the structural constraints of poster printing and display that, for him at least, helped direct the design process towards a specific creative outcome. He was careful to distinguish the activity of design from that of the artist-painter, whom he considered to be primarily concerned with self-expression.

Against this backdrop of continuous technical development it is worth describing the major staging-posts in the technical development of poster printing. This is valuable for a number of reasons. As Tom Eckersley made clear in his own book about poster design, the poster is always constrained by issues of market, display and production. The diagram that describes the intersection of these constraints might also begin, he thought, to direct the thinking towards a solution to the problem.

The appearance of the modern poster during the 1860s created a sensation. The colour, scale and expressive power of the poster were greeted enthusiastically from the very first. The public responded to the explicit modernity of the poster and to the expressive visual representations made possible by lithography. At a more subliminal level, the public also attached meanings of excitement and renewal to these images.

The modern poster was the first form of image produced that was designed to be seen dynamically, while moving, and from a distance. In simple terms this was made possible through its primary characteristics of scale, colour and sparkle. A secondary characteristic of the modern poster, facilitated through the technological developments listed above, has been the combination of image and text elements into a single unified entity.

The modern poster was developed in the 1860s as a consequence of an opportunity afforded by the architectural evolution of the panoptic city and the modern spectacular. For the first time wider streets and continuous urban redevelopment combined with the aggregation, production and consumption of people and goods to provide the surplus that underpins our present-day consumer environment.

Eckersley always acknowledged that the graphic designer needed the complementary skills of technical colleagues to achieve the best results. At LCP, he was able to work with printer colleagues of the highest level.

The first stage of modern poster history was distinguished by the inclusion, in almost all posters, of a realistic depiction of the product being advertised. Artists such as John Hassall and Dudley Hardy became expert at placing realistically rendered products against a much more loosely painted field. This visual organisation, with its implicit hierarchy, became the default setting for much advertising and commercial art.

It is not surprising that, in the circumstances of the cultural sociology of the late nineteenth century, posters should have been attractive to many artists. The poster offered an accessible alternative to the exclusive, closed-off and aesthetically limited, salon-type environment of art connoisseurship with its associated cadre of gatekeepers.

For younger, more radical artists the poster offered a democratic and inexpensive way of making images. The avant-garde embraced the poster as a means of escaping the constricted bourgeois values of the museum and gallery. Furthermore, the poster aligned itself formally with the street and with the dynamic and anarchic values of the metropolitan spectacular.

The success of the poster quickly created a market for display sites. The rents for display space were, from the first, carefully calibrated according to advertising demand and footfall. The control of these lucrative sites, by commercial landlords, was bolstered by legislation outlawing the fly-posting of posters. The regulation of poster display appealed to social conservatives who considered the poster an environmental eyesore and associated advertising images with a Babylonian excess of materialism and consumption.

Colour Lithography

All printing is a form of magic, but lithography is especially impressive. It seems improbable and incomprehensible until one sees it demonstrated.

Lithography was invented, or discovered, at the end of the eighteenth century in Germany, by Alois Senefelder. The starting point for the development of lithography had been a search for an economical form of printing that could combine traditional letterforms with different kinds of visual elements and mark-making.

Traditionally, images had been produced by the inclusion of either *intaglio* (sunken) or relief blocks within the letterpress page. The scale of images was therefore limited to the prevailing page sizes of letterpress printing. The small scale of wood-block illustration, by Thomas Bewick for example, produced exquisite effects of black and white sparkle on the page. But these were not generally images that suited the sight lines and accelerations of modern life.

Lithography exploited the antipathy of oil and water to mark out a design on a flat surface. The design was drawn, using a special grease, onto the prepared flat surface. Ink could then be applied so that it would adhere to the grease and be washed away from the remaining surface of the stone. A print could then be taken from the inked stone by bringing paper into contact with it. In contrast to the traditional mechanics of printing, the lithographic press eschewed pressure, preferring to bring paper into the briefest contact with the prepared design.

The relative absence of pressure from the lithographic process suddenly allowed for different mechanical forces to be exploited in printing. Pressure could, eventually, be replaced by rotation and speed. Furthermore, and most significantly, lithography suddenly allowed for a much larger printing surface.

In the traditional printing press, the downward force of the press is used to squeeze ink and paper together. The mechanical design of the letterpress printing machine is such that the downward forces of the press are quickly dissipated towards the edges of the platen. In practical terms, this has tended to limit the scale of illustrated material that could be printed. This was especially the case because of the additional costs associated with producing engraved or cut plates for illustration.

By a happy coincidence, the perfect support for lithographic printing was found to be a limestone, quarried from southern Germany close to where Senefelder was working.

The great virtue of stone as the support for lithography was that it was entirely resistant to the large amount of water involved in the process and was robust enough to withstand the vagaries of manhandling around the workshop. Also, the stones could be prepared in large sizes and could be either saved for subsequent printing, or reground and used again.

In its earliest and most rudimentary form, lithography found an immediate use in the printing of sheet music. The foundation skill of drawing in lithography also made the new process especially attractive to itinerant and topographical artists.

Colour lithography quickly developed so that complex and realistic images could be created through the addition and overprinting of separate colours. To create a complete design, each constituent colour required its own printing. For complex images, the picture would have to be broken down into its constituent colours and a stone prepared for the printing of each colour.

The printing process of lithography simply involved, in the first instance, the bringing together of paper and ink. The removal (for all practical purposes) of pressure in the printing process allowed for several substantial developments on the kinds of prints that could be produced. They could be made bigger, the engineering of the presses could be simplified, and the process transformed from one of pressure to one of rolling speed. This eventually allowed for the development of powered presses which, in turn, allowed for faster operation and increased efficiency.

Distinguished by its combination of drawing, scale, stone, and a powered rolling action, lithography provided an efficient, economical and flexible range of outcomes. This was attractive to industrial manufacturers, who could now produce packaging, point-of-sale notices and advertising for their products. The history of lithography is one of industrially scaled production, usually allied to a large-scale regional manufacturer.

Lithography was also attractive to new types of service providers, notably the railways, where the techniques of lithography could be used to present detailed numerical information in tabular form. The printing of railway timetables was, for example, very complex in letterpress form. Lithography allowed for the presentation of new types of data associated with the acceleration and growth of the machine-ensemble. All of this helped to establish colour lithography as the pre-eminent form of printing for the industrial economy, and the machine-ensemble, of the late nineteenth century.

The study of nineteenth-century colour lithographic printing reveals that extraordinary effort and care went into the elaboration of these printed images. Often, the finished print might require the preparation of twenty or so different stones. Obviously, the time and resources required for the elaboration and make-ready of these prints was such that colour lithography was only really economical for larger print runs.

The capital investment required for the machinery associated with automated presses also placed colour lithography beyond all but the largest regional concerns. For the larger printers of industrial packaging, the stones could be saved and reused at intervals as required. Alternatively, the stones could be cleaned and used for a different product.

In a typical late nineteenth-century lithographic print factory, the press would be centre stage and surrounded by workshops preparing stones, trimming paper and so on. The economic logic of the print factory was to keep the press running as much as possible in order to cover the costs of start-up and development.

The techniques of lithographic drawing were progressively elaborated so that amazingly complex visual material could be printed. In its original form, lithographic drawing required the design to be reversed. The addition of an offset roller into the machine press allowed for a more straightforward translation of design into a positive.

By the end of the nineteenth century, print technicians had made a number of developments that had further extended the range of colour lithography. New coloured inks had been developed, in both opaque and transparent forms, that allowed the production of almost any visual effect, albeit at a cost of time and make-ready. Metal sheets had been elaborated as an economical alternative to the expensive and cumbersome stones. The metal plates could also be curved, so as to be fixed onto rollers, and to further increase the speed of the machine.

Perhaps the most significant technical development was that of the half-tone screen. This allowed for the mid-tones of photographic hues to be translated into the binary code of black and white for printing, and the process of translating images into print became increasingly mechanical through the incorporation of studios and dark-rooms into the print-works.

In general, lithographic printing was understood as a commercial activity and its engagement with the worlds of art and design was limited. Artistic lithography developed fitfully and remained relatively small-scale in contrast to the print factories associated with industrial-scale printing.

The translation of design into print was an activity defined principally by technical accuracy rather than expressive potential. The pictures for advertising were rendered by hand in the original and interpreted, by skilled print-work technicians, into a printed facsimile of the original. It hardly needs stating that the craft-based interpretation of the original artwork was time-consuming and expensive. The majority of commercial colour lithography from the late nineteenth century is technically precise without being very emotionally engaging.

During the early twentieth century, lithographers at the Central School of Arts and Crafts in London began to explore the expressive potential of the direct mark-making possible in lithography. Frank Pick, for one, was sensitive to the potential of these developments to produce a different type of advertising image.

Nevertheless, by the 1930s, when Tom Eckersley and Eric Lombers were designing posters for London Transport, Shell and the GPO, the relationships between patrons, printers and designers remained more or less what it had always been. That is, one of separate activities.

The technical staff of the print shop were at the forefront of efforts to improve the economics of printing through speed and efficiency; they made mechanical improvements to the press machinery – adding rollers and power to the press to speed it up. They also developed split duct printing, which allowed for two colours to be printed at a single pass through the machine, and were systematic in their documentation of effects made possible by overprinting. The technical manuals published by Thomas Griffits are the standard works on this subject.

At Salford School of Art, Eckersley and Lombers had learned to produce designs as hand-drawn and coloured artwork in actual size. This involved drawing, painting and air-brush work to produce something that the technicians at the print factory could translate to printed form. At this time, the techniques of poster design remained firmly aligned with those of fine art, with little consideration of typography, integration and space within the design.

The Lithographic Poster in Modern Life

The end of the First World War was marked by a period of economic, political and social upheaval in all of the combatant nations. The consequences of war played out differently within the various contexts of military defeat, economic ruin and political victory.

In Britain, these changes made themselves felt through the promises of 'homes for heroes' and in the extension of democratic rights to women. Design reform in the inter-war years was an expression, through materials and technology, of combined tangible and social benefit.

With its Great Power status confirmed by victory, the post-war period also saw the emergence in Britain of a new scale of enterprise with integrated systems and global reach. These organisations made use of the poster to communicate their services and intentions to an ever-wider public. The availability of these goods and services, made possible through the benefits of

Handles Protect Hands
Pat Keely for RoSPA, 1941
Paul and Karen Rennie Collection, Estate of Pat Keely

Tom Eckersley's role at RoSPA allowed him to help some of his
colleagues with commissions in the period after the Second World
War. Pat Keely was an almost exact contemporary of Eckersley
and a colleague at AGI.

No Room for Horseplay Here
H.A. Rothholz for RoSPA, 1944
Paul and Karen Rennie Collection, Estate of H.A. Rothholz

H.A. Rothholz was an emigré designer and colleague of
Tom Eckersley. The RoSPA campaigns made good use of
emigré designers working in Britain.

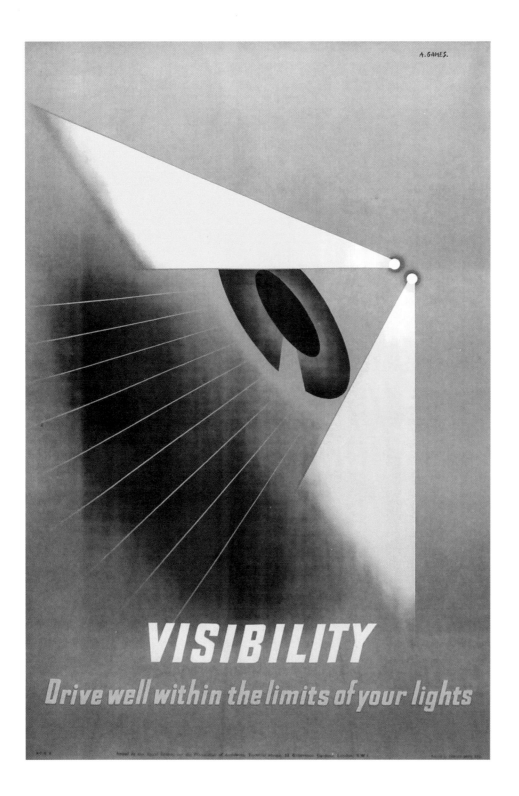

Visibility
Abram Games for RoSPA, 1947
Paul and Karen Rennie Collection,
Estate of Abram Games

Abram Games was well established as
the foremost poster designer in Britain
during the Second World War. The
use of his design gave extra weight to
RoSPA's road safety campaign.

productivity and economy, was equally understood as an expression of progress.

The advent of the First World War and the production of propaganda images marked the end of the first period of poster history. The second, modern period of poster design was distinguished by greater simplification and more pronounced scaling effects of typography and colour. Also, the mechanical processes of photography began to be integrated, through the half-tone and process block, into a single integrated typo-photo element.

In the 1920s and 1930s there remained considerable technical limitations to the integration of photographic elements into poster-scaled communications. The half-tone screens available to facilitate the printing of photographic tone remained crude and, when enlarged to poster sizes, the resulting images lacked clarity and detail. Artists and designers began to experiment with montage and collage effects to assemble larger photographic elements.

In Britain, designers such as Edward McKnight Kauffer were engaged in a series of visual experiments that sought to frame photographic elements within the established visual and painterly rhetoric of poster design.

The cultural phenomenon of modernism, in its twentieth-century context, has usually been associated with the specific period of cultural and political realignment following the First World War. The modernist project expressed itself differently according to the circumstances devolving from the military and political experience of the war.

The fitness for purpose and economy of materials associated with modern efficiency was also expressed through the visual culture of poster design. In their most

simplified and economical form the new posters, with their flat colour and geometric shapes, were understood as forms of abstraction. The ability, among ordinary people, to connect these abstracted shapes to the metropolitan experience of everyday life suggested the possibility of a visual language with increased symbolic potential.

Photo-mechanical and Offset Reproduction

The advent of the half-tone screen and the development of mechanical reproduction allowed for photographic elements to be increasingly used in the elaboration of designs for posters. During the 1930s, aspiring modernists such as Eckersley and Lombers had become familiar, through the international design press, with the graphic language of typo-photo and space. In terms of poster design the integration of half-tone elements posed a problem of scale. In practical terms it was difficult to enlarge photo-elements so that they worked at the scale of the larger posters, so designers developed ways of combining photographic elements through montage and by framing photo-elements within the established visual language of advertising. Eckersley and Lombers were at the forefront of these experiments.

The term 'photo-mechanical offset lithography' actually comprises two separate and distinct terms that describe the technology, process and specification of what is being done.

Offset lithography refers to a development of lithography whereby the addition of an offset roller into the print machinery allows for a simplification and acceleration of the printing process. The term 'offset' may be understood as distinguishing an up-to-date and efficient form of high-volume printing.

The two-colour lithographic press, for example, was a powered rotary press, fitted with offset rollers that allowed for two colours to be printed with a single pass through the machine. The machine comprises two plate cylinders. These are the cylinders to which the prepared metal litho plates are fixed. The metal plates, made from zinc or aluminium, are prepared and then formed to wrap around the plate cylinders. Each of the plate cylinders is paired with an offset cylinder. In addition to these large cylinders, there are a number of smaller rollers that pick up and distribute the ink evenly across the whole plate. In addition, a series of damping rollers are arranged so as to feed water, evenly and in just the right measure, across the full length of the plate cylinder. Water is a crucial part of the lithographic process, but also an element that needs very careful and precise control.

The arrangement of cylinders and rollers was generally stacked vertically to produce a machine with a compact footprint within the workshop. In contrast, four-colour, Heidelberg-style presses are usually laid out as a horizontal series of cylinders, one each for cyan, magenta, yellow and key (black) printings. Nowadays, this is known as CMYK.

The term photo-mechanical describes the process by which the make-ready of the printing plates is carried out according to a series of mechanical processes. That doesn't mean that the process is mechanised. It means that the tasks of the process are carried out according to technical norms and specifications. In the first instance, this allowed the work of colour separation to be done by using coloured filters. The interpretation of design according to subjective and craft judgement was replaced by a series of technical processes that could be exactly, and objectively, described by the numeric values of aperture settings and exposure associated with photography.

Putting all these terms together describes, to print technicians and graphic designers at least, a technical process and a standard of output that is defined by a series of mechanical steps. That doesn't mean that the process is entirely automated. But it does describe a process where each step is defined by numerically defined technical parameters rather than craft-based and subjective judgements. The precise expression of numeric values was understood as being explicitly precise, scientific and modern. It also made the print outcomes quicker and cheaper.

Despite the advancing automation of the print industry, there remained several areas of human expertise. In the print shop, machine minding was instrumental in the efficient running of the whole workshop. The success of any print enterprise requires that the machine presses are running at capacity. Any delay or stoppage in printing compromises the economic integrity of the works.

The basic roles of machine minding were to manage paper and ink so that speed and quality were optimised. Lithographic inks are usually supplied in the form of thick paste. This is thinned and then introduced into the machine via a trough located along the front of the machine. The inking rollers are arranged in sequence so that their action spreads the ink evenly across the full width of the machine. The ink must rest on the print so that it dries quickly and minimises the risk of offset, or of prints sticking to each other. Machine speed, efficiency and print quality were each linked to this ostensibly simple but important action.

Depending on the design of the poster, the ink trough could also provide a means for printing additional colours through the so-called split duct process. This involved dividing the ink trough through the erection of a partition across the trough. Differently coloured inks could then be placed in the trough on each side of the partition, meaning two colours could be printed simultaneously in one pass through the machine at optimum speed. This meant a two-colour machine could be transformed into a three- or four-colour machine.

Obviously, this mechanical sleight of hand requires that the inks be kept separate, and this is reflected in the design of the poster. A number of RoSPA designers, Tom Eckersley and Leonard Cusden among them, became adept at working to this specification.

The design of the poster was usually presented as painted artwork. This was prepared at actual size, or in the correct aspect ratio for enlargement to the standard size required. Photographic elements were included as collaged elements in the artwork.

The make-ready for printing involved preparing the colour separations and different plates required for printing. Each colour in the design required its own printing plate. The colour separations could be made relatively easily, using the photo studio, coloured filters and the darkroom. The separation could then be transferred to a thick glass plate and the design permanently rendered in liquid opaque. These glass plates, in actual size, could be retained for subsequent printings.

Laying the glass over a zinc printing plate with a prepared light-sensitive film and exposing it to light allowed for a precise transfer of the design, in actual size by contact, to be made quickly. This process is familiar to anyone who has worked in a black-and-white darkroom.

The finishing of the posters allowed for any trimming and folding operations. The posters were usually folded twice so they could be easily stored, identified and sent out in standard-sized postal envelopes.

These developments greatly expanded the scope of graphic design so that by the 1960s system, structure, process and identity had become more and more closely aligned.

The application of digital computers to this process has integrated each of these elements into a seamless digital stream comprising image, text, movement and sound. Nowadays, the term communication design refers to a cultural production that extends beyond the print economy.

The Offset Poster and Modern Life

The Second World War had an enormous impact on mass visual culture. The war quickly became an opportunity to express emancipatory political ideals and objectives that, as part of the concept of 'total war', were presented as legitimate war aims. The alignment of duty, sacrifice and social democracy became mythologised as the egalitarian experience of the war. This was expressed visually through the cultural phenomenon of the 'illustrated war'.

For practical purposes, the advertising economy collapsed during the war. The diversion of resources towards military production and the rationing of goods meant that the normal rules of consumption were abandoned. Nevertheless, the Second World War was significant, in Britain at least, for advancing graphic communication in two significant ways.

The scale and urgency of the propaganda requirements of total war effectively produced a paradigm shift within the visual print industry. The production of posters became a matter of urgency and work moved to smaller firms equipped with the machinery of mechanical reproduction. The transition to mechanical reproduction also transformed the creative role of the artist into one of technocratic specification and direction. So, 1939 marked the beginnings of a different type of creative activity in Britain.

The communication design of the Second World War combined the economies of modern design with the potential of surrealist association. The most significant poster designers of the Second World War began to combine visual elements and ideas into a single conceptual synthesis of an idea. Tom Eckersley, along with his contemporary and poster-designer colleague Abram Games, were recognised as masters of this synthesis.

The use of humour to engage the viewer was an important and unique development in the government propaganda of war, reconstruction and welfare. This use of humour in communication wasn't new. Within the context of war, though, it allowed propaganda communication to move beyond the fear and anxiety associated with the default settings of atrocity propaganda. The juxtapositions of surrealism allowed for the replacement of feelings of anxiety and fear with something more like black humour. Later, this potential would be appropriated by the advertising industry and its promotion of feelings associated with desire.

Post-war Printing
Several things happened in the later 1950s and 1960s that transformed the social fabric of Britain. For the first time since the war, young people had disposable income. The emergence of youth culture, founded on socially transgressive behaviour and principally expressed through music and fashion, opened a social space defined, in the first instance, by not becoming your parents.

The refusal to be limited by family finances or class origins was understood as an expression of social mobility. The ambitious scale of post-war meritocratic reform was exemplified by the extension of technical education as the end of military National Service transformed the student population. It immediately became younger and less deferential. For most of their history, university institutions had been a mechanism of assimilation into a social elite.

The massive expansion of the university sector began to change the student experience. The new 'plate glass' universities promoted education, through the methodologies of social science, as a process of interrogation and integration, rather than assimilation. By the far the most important change in the student population was derived from the equality of access given, for the first time, to female students. Suddenly the student population was gender-balanced.

It's not entirely surprising that, in these circumstances, the 1960s should end in the great political upheavals of 1968 and the various social experiments associated with sexual liberation and collective ownership.

By the middle of the 1960s, the student population was bigger, younger, more mixed, and increasingly angry. All this expressed itself through a variety of political campaigns and through the youthquake's lifestyle choices of loud music, fashion, sexual liberation and recreational drug use.

Good Stacks
Leonard Cusden for RoSPA, 1960s
Paul and Karen Rennie Collection,
Estate of Leonard Cusden

Leonard Cusden was Tom Eckersley's closest
colleague at RoSPA and, later, at LCP.

Asking for Trouble
Leonard Cusden for RoSPA, 1960s
Paul and Karen Rennie Collection,
Estate of Leonard Cusden

Please Keep Britain Tidy
Reginald Mount for the Central Office of
Information, 1960s
Paul and Karen Rennie Collection,
Estate of Reginald Mount

Reginald Mount worked with the Central
Office of Information on a wide-ranging
series of Government communications.

The lifestyle choices of the counter-revolution required their own forms of communication, and these were provided by the advent of modern screen printing. The development of the photo-optical process of make-ready in screen-print allowed for the process to become first choice for short-run and local print requirements … ideal for campus or college societies and events.

At a very basic level, screen printing is suitable where the results require a print run of fewer than, say, 200 copies; a design with solid blocks of colour but not so much fine detail; printing larger than A3 size; and designs that may be applied to T-shirts etc. Furthermore, much of the equipment required for printing could be home-made and the printing done on the floor (like at Warhol's Factory for example).

During the 1960s and 1970s, the internal screen-print culture of the London College of Printing provided a forcing ground of causes and styles, which were then appropriated by and integrated into the consumer culture of 'Swinging London'.

In its original form, screen printing was derived from stencil, or pochoir, printing, where ink was squeezed through a stencil and onto the paper. The Second World War had made stencil lettering graphically familiar. The problem with using paper or card stencils is that, over time and in relation to the number of prints taken, the stencils become wet and the design sharpness is compromised through damage.

It was possible to cut metal stencils, but these were relatively expensive. Another solution was to mount the stencil onto a framed screen so as to keep the stencil design sharp.

Until the 1950s, screens were cut by hand. This was a time-consuming, craft-based skill and made screen printing unsuitable for commercial purposes. At the end of the 1950s, however, the same kinds of technical developments that had transformed offset lithography into a series of mechanical operations began to apply themselves to screen printing.

The choice of stencil material is made in relation to the required print run and the materials available to hand. Cut-paper stencils are simple to make and can work well for very short-run printing. Film stencils are stronger and will last longer. Photo stencils, where the mesh, stencil and design are fused together, may last almost indefinitely.

Screen printing requires no additional equipment beyond the screen and frame. The frame may be placed onto the paper and a print made. Assuming the area is clean and level, it would even be possible to make a print from the floor.

Since every print is effectively printed separately, the organisation of print and paper around the workshop is very important. The studio doesn't require lots of space. However, it must have wet and dry areas, and is best served with a printing surface at about waist height. One of the biggest practical problems is making sure that completed prints are allowed to dry without becoming damaged or disfigured. The easiest way to do this originally would have been to hang the prints to dry from a washing-line across the studio.

Needless to say, it wasn't long before specialist technical equipment was available for printing and drying. This greatly simplified the actions required to make a print and speeded the whole process up.

Print manufacturers were quick to develop a range of inks to support the growing interest in screen printing. Inks were available in both oil- and water-based forms. The oil-based inks tended to be understood as professional-standard inks that allowed for a thicker and more dense perception of colour. The solid surface of the oil-based screen prints is one of the principal joys of appreciating these kinds of print. It wasn't surprising that colour merchants extended the range of available colours to include exciting fluorescent effects.

Water-based inks now dominate the student and amateur printing environments. The absence of powerful solvents in the water-based process means that health and safety can be maintained without the need for expensive vapour-extraction systems.

If screens are required to be reused with a different design, they can be washed clean and the fixed positive design removed. This usually involves washing the screen with solvents. Once all the hardened film has been removed, the screen and frame may be stored, ready to be reused.

When the National Theatre moved to London's South Bank in 1976, its posters were screen-printed. The designs, by Kenneth Briggs and others, produced a body of graphic work entirely in keeping with and in colourful counterpoint to the Brutalist architecture of Denys Lasdun's building and the imaginative and adventurous programming on the South Bank.

In Paris, during the student upheavals of 1968, screen prints became a visible expression of radical idealism. The display of posters, renewed every night and in flagrant disregard for various by-laws, provided clear evidence of civil disobedience. The posters also provided a visible counter to the prevailing order and tidiness of Parisian bourgeois quartiers.

The screen print quickly emerged as a significant cultural phenomenon at every level. In fine art,

screen-printed images became a staple of the pop art movement in America (with Andy Warhol, for example) and in the UK (Chris and Rose Prater's Kelpra Studio and Advanced Graphics, among others).

In 1968, the silk-screen poster gave visual expression to the student protest movement in France through the work of the Atelier Populaire. In the UK, the screen print aligned itself with a slightly different form of politics derived from countercultural hedonistic libertarianism. In popular cultural terms, the screen print became a staple of student bedrooms, notably through Hapshash and the Coloured Coat (Michael English and Nigel Waymouth).

In December 1966 English and Waymouth were introduced by the co-founders of the UFO Club on Tottenham Court Road. The pair worked well together and they set up a small studio in Holland Park, close to the offices of the notorious Oz magazine. The posters were then printed and distributed by Osiris Visions, owned by the *International Times*, in the basement of the Indica Bookshop in Mason's Yard, St James's.

The social and political transformations of the 1960s counter-culture, and of Swinging London especially, were built upon a greatly expanded range of print outcomes. These included illustrated books, magazines, carrier bags and vastly more consistent forms of corporate identity.

Philosophically, the powerful distinction between the status of word and image seemed to be collapsing, or was at least becoming more fluid.

The British countercultural alignment of ideas and hedonism continued in the 1970s with the nihilist chaos of punk, derived from earlier Dada experiments, and in the 1980s with the transcendent potential of rave culture and Ibiza.

The Ideas Poster

The technical development of the modern poster through its various stages of colour lithography, offset and mechanical reproduction, and screen printing has attempted to accelerate the production of posters through speed of printing and economies in the time required for make-ready. In addition, the broad direction of aesthetic evolution associated with these developments has been away from the complexities of craft-based and time-consuming handicraft processes.

The tendency to economy, implicit in the visual simplifications described in the process above, also supported a move towards a more abstracted visual language of colour and form. In turn, this provided an opportunity for the evolution of an ideas-based visual language able to express a wider range of messages to a greater proportion of the population.

Tom Eckersley's career began in the period of 'pictures for advertising' and extended into a period that witnessed the enormous extension in scope of the kinds of messages to which graphic and communication could be applied. He was instrumental in driving this extension through the example of his work for organisations such as RoSPA.

Eckersley's own design formation, at Salford in the early 1930s, introduced him to the international masters of poster design. In the late 1930s, he and Eric Lombers established themselves as poster designers and worked with such contemporary luminaries as Edward McKnight Kauffer and Austin Cooper. Eckersley used the example provided by successful poster design to develop his own ideas and to build upon this foundation.

Power: Position, Scale and Point of View

It is usual to begin by positioning the main subject of the poster in the centre of the design. This frames the subject; but it can lack dynamism and drama, so the subject may be moved so that it is ranged, left or right, up or down, within the frame.

Obviously, the scale of the main subject in the design provides an important clue as to its significance. Usually, we recognise scale as an important signifier of status. In conjunction with position, this should draw the eye to what is important in the design.

The poster provides a frame (or window) to the view. By bringing the frame closer to the subject, we can make the subject appear larger. This adds significance. At its most extreme, we can move so close to the subject that the frame can no longer contain the whole subject, and the subject bleeds beyond the edge of the poster.

Suddenly, the subject can be understood as extending beyond the frame of the view; this implicit perception makes any subject seem much more significant. If the image crop makes the subject seem bigger, the resulting effect can be monumental.

Nowadays, everyone is familiar with this idea from the cropping of digital images. But, until relatively recently, these considerations would have seemed arcane to all but a few professional pictorial technicians. The advent of high-quality and portable photographic cameras (the Leica 35mm viewfinders in the 1920s, for example) allowed for a new approach to photography, where the photographer framed the picture in the viewfinder. The advent of photographic art direction in fashion magazines also developed these ideas. Before the Second World War, the modern poster was a proving ground for the professional development behind this kind of design decision-making.

The frame could also be tilted. This provided for a point of view that could be elevated or lowered. Both of these options carried significant implications. The bird's-eye view gave the observer a larger and more expansive view of the composition. Also, feelings of soaring freedom and excitement could be provoked by the hint of vertigo implicit in these elevated perspectives.

Conversely, a lowered point of view could make the subject seem to tower over the viewer. This provided dramatic monumentality, but at the cost of potentially intimidating the viewer. This very powerful perspective was often used so as to produce the domineering images associated with political propaganda. It was also useful in conveying the scale of medieval ruins or modern industrial plant.

Flat Colour

The main skill associated with simplification was to choose the appropriate range of colours so that the subject could be rendered successfully. The choice of colours had to combine naturalism with contrast. Furthermore, the architecture of the design had to be considered so as to lead the eye into the obviously two-dimensional picture plane. The '2D-flat-colour-into-3D-space' design trick is achieved by carefully using small areas of black to guide the eye into the space. The black is traditionally the last colour to be printed and effectively combines all the colours into a single spatial arrangement. You can observe the effectiveness of this in the posters of both Tom Purvis and Frank Newbould.

Austin Cooper, designer and principal of the Reimann School of Design, London, described the 'carry' of

various colours. This was a function of tone and contrast and, crucially, allowed the poster to attract attention over distance.

By the 1930s, colour theory, Gestalt psychology and print had combined so that both the science and meaning of colour were understood. Tom Eckersley had understood this well: 'The good designer can achieve far more with two colours than the poor one with twelve, since it is not the number of colours you use but the way in which you employ them which governs the result.'

Sparkle and Pattern

Power and economy are not enough, though, in poster design. The design also has to have an element of sparkle to attract the eye. This is a form of optical disturbance equivalent to a fluttering movement of light. It's this apparent movement that catches the eye. We also understand this optical effect as a kind of energy, which we find attractive.

Traditionally, printers and designers have exploited the inherent appeal of sparkle in letterforms and typography. You can see this clearly in early nineteenth-century letterpress playbills and notices, which draw the eye towards the most pronounced contrast of light and dark.

At the beginning of the nineteenth century, most local printers were traditional letterpress printers. Notices about theatrical entertainments and local events were elaborated entirely from the available stock of metal or wooden type in various styles and sizes. Most printers carried a relatively limited range of type styles and sizes, with relatively few styles in large sizes, meaning it was nearly always impossible to print these kinds of text-based notices in the single and consistent typographic style with which we are familiar today.

Printer-designers made a virtue of this impossibility by elaborating notices in a variety of styles and sizes.

The creation of a vibrant contrast between the blacks and white of the print was made possible by exploiting the differences between various letterforms; italic, shadow and fat-face letters were each used in close proximity and in different sizes and weights. Elements of this design tradition may be seen in the earliest railway posters produced in the nineteenth century, and in the typographic and psychological experiments of the 1960s counterculture.

By the 1920s and 30s, new considerations of typographic consistency were being demanded by larger organisations determined to be more consistent in the expression of their corporate identity. Monotype machines made the consistent presentation of type across all the various printed products of an organisation possible.

In poster design, the letterforms were usually hand-drawn. Indeed, the technical skills of accurate letter drawing provided a platform for the development of the commercial artist. During the 1920s and 1930s, large-scale sans serif letterforms were elaborated as exemplifying the characteristics of power and economy, identified above.

For Eckersley, design considerations were always linked to those of economy and purpose. Far from considering these issues as constraints, he always described them in terms of shaping the design process constructively and, to a certain extent, providing the key to the best solution to the problem being considered.

Economy

Tom Eckersley was always conscious of economy as a guiding principle of design. In part this reflected the commercial reality of costs that framed the design process. But he was also concerned with conceptual economy and the simplification of ideas and reduction of technical complexities so as to achieve the maximum impact and meaning with the minimum of means. This was an idea famously espoused by his colleague and contemporary Abram Games.

Tom always promoted ideas and economy as the foundations of good design. His *Poster Design* (1954) makes the point that the technical formation of the designer is there to support a variety of outcomes as part of an iterative process. In the end, though, it is most likely that the final choice between possible outcomes will be determined by the economic constraints set by the client.

But, for Eckersley, economy was never just about cost. He used the term to describe the process of simplification, and of how to achieve more with less. Of course, simplicity and economy have been guiding principles in every aspect of art and design during the twentieth century. Eckersley applied this thinking to both the typographic- and image-based part of the design, but also to the space in which these elements were placed. The area around these pictorial elements became an active and dynamic space in which viewer and object were placed in relation to each other.

Economy and standardisation combined to defenestrate the great variety of type in favour of a logic of modern efficiency and economy. Nevertheless, all these elements combined to impact on both the environments and people of the modern world.

How Posters Survive

Posters aren't usually made to survive. Indeed, they are made to be pasted up. The posters thus pasted are lost forever. The posters that survive have usually been saved by the designer, printer or some other enthusiast. The majority of posters in this book conform to this pattern.

Nearly every image in the book originates from Tom's own studio archive. Tom was scrupulous in retaining proof copies of all of his designs. Some of these were kept in plan chests, some were pasted onto board for display purposes, and some were even laminated onto hardboard.

The collector and poster enthusiast Herbert Robinson had met Tom Eckersley through his connection with the Camden Art Centre. At some point, probably in the late 1980s or early 1990s, Herbert was able to purchase a large number of posters from Tom.

My own interest in Tom Eckersley began in the 1980s when I started to collect posters. I recall that our first Eckersley purchase was of Scientists Prefer Shell from 1936 … We have kept collecting and saving material by Tom Eckersley whenever we have found it. Later, we were introduced to Tom by his friend, colleague and contemporary Abram Games. I interviewed them both for a design magazine in the early 1990s.

In 1996, Sotheby's offered a collection of posters from Tom's studio. This sale was not a success. Later, some of these posters were introduced to the market.

At about the same time, a large quantity of poster material was gifted to the London College of Printing, now the London College of Communication and part of the University of the Arts, London. This collection is now identified as The Eckersley Archive and held within the library at the college. This archive forms the basis of much of the work in this book.

Poster Sizes

The modern poster is distinguished by the characteristics of its scale and colour. Paradoxically, the large size of posters works against their being easily preserved; they are difficult to store and they are easily damaged. As a consequence of this, most posters that survive are double crown (20 x 30in) or double royal (25 x 40in) size. The quad crown (50 x 40in) poster size of railway advertising is about the largest form of poster that survives in Britain. The posters from Tom Eckersley's studio are mostly from these sizes.

Bibliography

Books by (or illustrated by) Tom Eckersley

Cabrelly, E.A., *Animals on Parade* (1948), London, Conrad

Eckersley, D., *Cat O' Nine Lives* (1946), London, Peter Lunn

Eckersley, T., *Poster Design* (1954), London, Studio

Exhibition catalogues, magazines and books with work by Tom Eckersley

Artist Partners, *Prospectus 1* (1954), London, Dover Street

Artist Partners, *Prospectus 2* (1958), London, Dover Street

Camden Arts Centre, *Tom Eckersley – Posters and Other Works* (1980), London, CAAT

Gebrauchsgraphik, Vol. 21/2, *Warning Signs* (1950), Munich, Wittkop

Gebrauchsgraphik, No. 9, *Tom Eckersley* (1959), Munich, Bruckmann

Graphis, No. 14, *Special Number – England* (1946), Zurich, Amstutz & Herdeg

Graphis, No. 31, *British Commercial Art* (1950), Zurich, Amstutz & Herdeg

Graphis, No. 56/56, *Tom Eckersley* (1954), Zurich, Amstutz & Herdeg

London Institute, *Tom Eckersley – His Graphic Work* (1994), London, London Institute LCP

Society of Industrial Artists, *Designers in Britain 1* (1947), London, Wingate

Society of Industrial Artists, *Designers in Britain 2* (1949), London, Wingate

Society of Industrial Artists, *Designers in Britain 3 (Festival)* (1951), London, Wingate

Triggs, T., and Rennie, P., *Tom Eckersley* (2005), London, London College of Communication

General Reference

Artmonsky, R., and Preston, D., *Tom Purvis* (2014), London, Artmonsky Arts

Briggs, A., *Victorian Cities* (1971), Harmondsworth, Pelican

Brumwell, M., *Bright Ties Bold Ideas* (2010), Truro, Tie Press

Henrion, F.H.K., *AGI Annals* (1989), Zurich, AGI

Hill, C., *Society and Puritanism* (1969), London, Panther

Hill, C., *The World Turned Upside Down* (1975), London, Penguin

Hill, C., *Puritanism and Revolution* (1986), London, Peregrine

Hillier, B., *Projecting Britain* (1982), London, BFI

Hunt, T., *Building Jerusalem* (2004), London, Weidenfeld & Nicolson

James, L., *Print and the People* (1976), London, Allen Lane

Joyce, P., *The Rule of Freedom* (2003), London, Verso

Lambert, F., *Graphic Design Britain* (1967), London, Peter Owen

Main, P., *Peter Lunn: Children's Publisher* (2010), Stirling, Lomax

McAlhone, B., Stuart, D., Quinton, G., and Asbury, N., *A Smile in the Mind* (2015), London, Phaidon

Poyner, R., ed., *Communicate* (2004), London, Barbican

Ritchie, B., *A Touch of Class: The Story of Austin Reed* (1990), London, James & James

Rennie, P., *Design – GPO Posters* (2010), Woodbridge, ACC

Rennie P., *Modern British Posters* (2010), London, BDP

Rennie P., *Safety First* (2016), Glasgow, Saraband

Thompson, B., *Devastating Eden* (2004), London, Harper Collins

Treweek, C., and Zeitlyn, J., *The Alternative Printing Handbook* (1983), Harmondsworth, Penguin

Wilson, C., *Richard Hollis Designs for the Whitechapel* (2017), London, Hyphen

Thanks

As I've already mentioned, I seem to have been writing about Tom Eckersley for some time. I've been able to do this because of the help and support of a number of people, and I am very grateful to them all.

Tom's sons, Anthony, Richard and Paul, were each supportive of my interest in Tom from the beginning. Now, the younger members of the family have extended their help and support, as much as possible, to this project.

Paul Eckersley's position at the London College of Printing facilitated the creation in the early 1990s of the Eckersley Archive. It was my good fortune to be appointed Eckersley Archivist at LCP by Liz Leyland, Dean of the School of Graphic Design. The school has always been supportive of my efforts at presenting parts of Tom's story and of sharing the work with students and staff colleagues.

The Eckersley Archive is now housed in the Research Centre of the Library Collections at the London College of Communication. I am grateful to Sarah Mahurter and her colleagues for all their help with this project over the years.

My academic supervisors, Janice Hart and Jeremy Aynsley, helped me transform the research I'd done into RoSPA's Second World War industrial safety campaign into a coherent story. When I started this research, before the internet became widespread, I was required to assemble an archive from the disparate holdings of various museums. It was a bit surprising to discover, over the course of the project, that RoSPA had very little sense of their own history, nor of the quality and significance of their poster campaigns. I shared the outcomes of my research with RoSPA and gave them a little more context for their important and continuing work.

I was delighted, in 2010, to receive an unexpected telephone call from RoSPA saying that they had discovered an archive of posters and artwork in an old warehouse in Birmingham. The discovery of the archive allowed for a more detailed account of their poster campaigns to become part of the RoSPA centenary celebration of 2017. The poster archive is now housed in the new Library of Birmingham.

It's one thing to have a particular interest of one's own. It's quite another to find a partner who shares that interest and contributes to the project. I've been hugely lucky to have been supported throughout by Karen, my wife. We met, back in the day, looking at the same object and quickly began collecting things together. Karen has always been enthusiastic about Tom's posters and of the need to make them better known. Her support and enthusiasm has kept this show on the road.

Karen also helped me to enter the world of professional graphic design during the 1980s. I didn't become a designer, but I met Karen's sister Lynn Trickett, of Trickett and Webb. Lynn, too, was a big fan of Tom Eckersley's work and clarified for me why his combination of intelligence and technique was so valuable a legacy to the designers who came after.

My parents were artistic without, I think, being bohemian. They introduced me into a world, during the 1960s and 1970s, in which it was possible to combine art and life in ways that seemed to combine practical usefulness with moral intelligence. The implicit combination of practicality and philosophy evident in so much of Tom Eckersley's poster design was something that seemed familiar to me and would, I think, have chimed with my father's own professional practice as an architect.

Lastly, I would like to acknowledge the support, kindness and professionalism of my publishers, Pavilion Books. They, too, seem to have played a bigger part in my life than I first realised. The present-day Pavilion includes the imprint of Batsford books. I recognised the name Batsford from the distinctive flat-colour dust-wraps of their guidebooks, designed by Brian Cook, and from my childhood interest in chess publishing, with its specialised typographic code and presentation.

So, this book is …

For Ian, my father
For Lynn, my sister-in-law
and, of course, for Karen

Index

255

Picture credits

All pictures © The Estate of Tom Eckersley and the Eckersley Archive, London College of Communication, University of the Arts, London, except the following. Page 17: Classic Image / Alamy Stock Photo; 18 Private collection © Look and Learn/ Bridgeman Images; 22 Richerman, licensed under the Creative Commons Attribution-Share Alike 3.0 Unported license (https://creativecommons.org/licenses/by-sa/3.0/legalcode); 44 (top and bottom), 45 (top and bottom), 46, 47 (left and right), 171 © TfL from the London Transport Museum collection; 57, 65, 74, 75, 76, 77, 78, 79, 80, 81, 82, 83, 84, 85, 86, 87, 88 (left, centre and right), 89, 90, 92, 93, 94, 95, 96, 97, 98 © RoSPA; 63 Album / Alamy Stock Photo; 157, 158 (top and bottom) @diana_jarvis / Alamy Stock Photo; 237 (left) © Estate of Pat Keely; 237 (right) © Estate of H.A. Rothholz/Design Archives at the University of Brighton; 238 © Estate of Abram Games; 243 (left and right) © Estate of Leonard Cusden; 244 Crown Copyright.

All reasonable efforts have been taken to ensure that the reproduction of the content in this book is done with the full consent of the copyright owners. If you are aware of unintentional omissions, please contact the company directly so that any necessary corrections may be made for future editions.